Research Strategies

Research Strategies

Finding Your Way Through the Information Fog

William Badke

Writers Club Press
San Jose New York Lincoln Shanghai

Research Strategies
Finding Your Way Through the Information Fog

Writers Club Press
an imprint of iUniverse.com, Inc.

For information address:
iUniverse.com, Inc.
620 North 48th Street, Suite 201
Lincoln, NE 68504-3467
www.iuniverse.com

Cover art by Rosemary Badke
This book is a substantial revision of The Survivor's Guide to Library
Research (Grand Rapids: Zondervan Publishing House, 1990). Zondervan is
a division of HarperCollins.

ISBN: 0-595-10082-1

Printed in the United States of America

Contents

Preface ix

1 Taking Charge 1

    Wrestling with a Topic 2
    A Model for Research 6
    Getting Started in Research 6
    Finding a Good Question 9
    How About a Few Examples? 11

2 Databases 14

    The Next Stage 14
    Database Searching 15
    Some Final Hints 32

3 Blowing Away the Information Fog 34

    Finding your Way in an Information Hierarchy 35
    Strategies to Clear the Fog in the Book Collection 43

4 Making Your Way Through the Periodical Maze 50

    What Periodical Indexes Are All About 51
    A First Adventure with a Real Live Computerized Periodical Index 53
    Tips and Hints 59
    Inside the New World of Periodical Indexes 62
    Final Pep Talk 66

5 Internet Research 67

    A Brief Introduction to the Net 68
    Searching the Internet 73

Evaluating Information from the Internet 78
Some Internet Addresses Valuable for Research Purposes 81

6 Other Resources You May Not Have Considered 83

Seeing Where You've Been 83
Using ERIC 85
Government Documents 93
Library Catalogues Other Than Your Own 93
Doctoral Dissertations 94
Full Text Reference Tools 95

7 Case Studies in Research 96

"The Teenage Suicide Crisis" 96
"Lucrezia Borgia" 104

8 Learning How to Read for Research 109

Reading for the Connoisseur and the Glutton 109
Note Taking 116
Further Notes on Note-Taking 122
A Gentle Warning About the Horrible Crime of Plagiarism 123

9 Organizing Your Notes to Write your Paper 125

Your Notes 126
Your Bibliography 128
Your Subject Index 129
Indexing your Notes for Larger Assignments 131

10 Tips on Research Writing 133

The Outline 133
Some Tips on Research Writing 138

About the Author 149

Appendix One 151

Appendix Two 167

The Purpose of an Academic Library 167
The Parts of an Academic Library 168
Using the Library Catalogue 172
Signing Out Books 179
Some Words about Plagiarism 180
Some Final Advice 181

Preface

Everyone does research.

Some just do it better than others.

This book is definitely for you if you are:

❖ A university student whose term papers are patented as a cure for insomnia;

❖ A Dilbert of industry who's been told to do a feasibility study on the expansion potential of ice cream bar sales in Nome, Alaska;

❖ a simple honest citizen trying to find the truth behind the adverising so that the next car you buy won't be like the last one, that made you *persona non grata* at the automobile association;

Are you ready for your next research project? Really ready? Do you have the skills and strategies to get the job done efficiently and effectively without panic attacks and the need for a long vacation when you are done? Do you have confidence that you can start with a topic you know nothing about and end with an understanding of it that is neither trite nor superficial?

If not, this book is for you. Even if you have significant research skills, you can learn better ones if you take the time to read on

Learning how to do research does not have to be painful. It can be fun. Honestly. Personally, I have so much fun that my family has to kidnap me out of the library whenever they want to go on an outing or buy groceries. You can have the same joy that I have. Read on.

1

Taking Charge

You who are reading this book may be saying to yourself, "I've never been good at this. In fact, I don't think I have a good research project in me."

My response is, "Of course you don't. A good research project is out there, not inside you. What you have to do is get out there, find the data, work with it, and make it your own."

Now, before you run off to lurk in a dark alley frequented by black market sellers of data, let me offer you a safer alternative. What follows is a list of basic things that you need to have working for you in order to turn your anxiety into a brilliant project leading to an excellent product.

1. You need an intense desire to do a brilliant project, not just an average one. By definition, most people can do an average project.
2. You need to take your time and plan your research as a *strategy* rather than as a mad dash through libraries and databases. Libraries know when you have reached the panic stage. The books close ranks and refuse to be found. Titles in the catalogue trade places so that you can't locate them. The smell of musty books renders you numb and silly. Databases can do even worse things to you (don't ask).

Never panic. Take it easy. Work out a plan and show that data who's in charge here.

3.   You need to develop *lateral thinking.* Lateral thinking is akin to what happens in a football game: The quarterback has no openings at all. If he runs with the ball, he'll be flattened. So, instead of moving forward, he throws the ball sideways to another player who can move it forward. These are the steps:

❖ Recognize that your advance along one line is blocked.
❖ Abandon your approach and look for another that is completely different.
❖ Run with your new approach and make it work (or try yet another).

It's like the old story of the truck that got stuck in a highway underpass. No towing vehicle of any kind could get it out, and so the workers were left with the option of dismantling an expensive truck or tearing down an even more expensive underpass until…

…until the light bulb went on and some bright lateral thinker suggested letting the air out of the truck's tires to *lower* it. Lateral thinking works beyond the obvious,in the realm of the creative. Nurture this gift within you.

Wrestling with a Topic

"I'm writing a paper on the Lollards. I don't know who they are or were (and I'm finding it hard to care). When I'm done—if I can find anything in this confusing yet undersized library—I will have a research paper describing the Lollards. It will stress description of the Lollards. Its theme will be 'Describing the Lollards.' The point I will seek to make is that the Lollards can indeed be described."

Exciting, isn't it? Don't those old Lollards just thrill you to pieces? Not really. It's just another research project, as tedious as the last one you did. *Fact is, it isn't even research.*

"What?" you say. "Not research? I searched the library catalogue and periodical indexes and even the Internet, and I've got a ton of stuff here. Don't tell me I'm not doing research."

All right, I won't. Go ahead and write your paper and describe your Lollards. Turn it in and wait for your professor to read the thing and give you the usual dreary mark. Obviously, you don't like your prof anyway, and that's why you keep doing this too him or her. Professors are no strangers to the kinds of boredom you inflict on them. In fact they're almost used to the tedious task of marking your essays. You bore the professor, and the professor pays you back by giving you a C. Any illusion that you actually did research will be dead by the time you get the essay back.

Not wanting to be harsh without giving you some help, let me ask: What is genuine research if it's not what you've been passing off? Let's begin by looking at what it is not.

Elements of False Research

➤ False research assumes that the task is to gather data and synthesize it. Thus the typical student "research" project involves amassing data, reading and absorbing it, then regurgitating it back onto a fresh piece of paper (sorry for the disgusting image).

➤ False research deals in generalities and surveys. It loves a superficial look at a big topic, and it abhors depth and analysis.

➤ False research asks no questions and makes no pretense at advancing knowledge. It is content to report on what has already been done, to summarize the past.

➤False research is so boring to the researcher that it's amazing that it ever gets completed, let alone foisted on the longsuffering professor.

The Key to Genuine Research

What's the point of doing research? A flip answer might be that a professor or employer told you to, and you're just following orders. But that's not the answer I'm looking for.

Consider this dilemma as an example: A few years ago you bought a car that was a disaster. Its maker should have been executed for delusions of adequacy. While most cars have water dripping out of the exhaust pipe, yours had lemonade. You spent so much time pushing it that you were able to qualify for the weightlifting competition at the next Olympics. Your mechanic added a new wing onto his house with the money you spent keeping it on the road. Now you're due for a new vehicle, and you are not about to be stung again. So what to you do?

Research!!

You pick up every consumer reporting and car testing book or magazine you can find. You ask your friends. You go on the Internet. Why? Because you have a burning question to answer, and somewhere out there is the data you need to answer it.

This is what research is all about. The key to genuine research is *a good question*. Without a question, nothing you are doing can be called research. Just as your search through car books is driven by the query, "Which car should I buy this time?" so any research project worthy of its name is driven by a single research question.

What constitutes a good question? Here the situation becomes a bit more complex, because you need to begin rethinking the whole research process. Let me suggest the following steps:

Hardly Ever Accept a Topic as Given

Later in this chapter, we will consider the actual processes involved in getting a topic ready for research, but for now we need an overview of the basic principles. The first of these is that most any research project presented to you needs some work before it is viable enough to use.

Assume, first of all that the topic is probably too broad to be workable unless you're planning to write a book. A topic like the Lollards or abortion or economic conditions in Russia today is not likely to inspire depth of analysis because you don't have space in ten or twenty pages to deal with anything but the superficial. You are going to have to focus on a more narrow aspect of the topic so that you can deal with it in depth. Consider a bathtub with a gallon of water in it as opposed to a bathroom sink with a gallon of water in it. Which is deeper? The sink, because its borders are narrower. The same principle works in a research project—the narrower your focus, the more chance you have of getting some depth into your project.

Assume, second, that you are going to have to develop a sound working knowledge of the topic before you're going to know what to do with it.

Assume, third, that you're going to have to negotiate with the one who gave you the project. You need to know that what you propose is going to fly with the person ultimately responsible for your fate. But cheer up—professors are generally thrilled with some tiny evidence of creativity in their students. Go to your professor and ask politely, "Would you mind if I pursued *this* issue raised by the Lollards? It looks really interesting."

Your professor's heart will turn to mush and he or she will say quietly, "Yes, all right," while inside he or she is shouting, "A new approach! I'm getting a new approach!"

Caution: Don't ever say, "May I write on the Albigenses instead?" This signals the professor that you don't like the Lollards, and you most certainly will end up having to write on the Lollards anyway.

A Model for Research

What, then, is research all about? Here's a model:

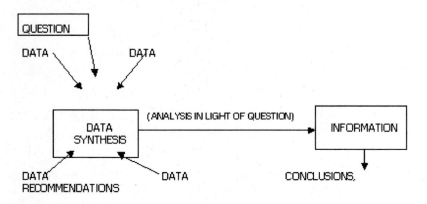

Explanation? You begin with a question, you collect data, you synthesize it, you analyze it in light of the question (leading to information), and then you come up with conclusions and recommendations. Look's easy, doesn't it? Maybe not, but we are about to embark on a journey that will make things much more clear.

Getting Started in Research

Getting a Working Knowledge through Reference Sources

Before you run off in all directions at once (like a draw-and-quarter competition at the local jousting match), get a grip on yourself. As I librarian, I see the same painful experience repeated day after day—students walking fearfully into our book stacks area, then stopping, frozen to the ground.

I know what's buzzing through their battered minds—"I'm here, I'm actually here in the library, about to start researching my topic, and I don't have a *clue* what to do. Time has stopped, and people are staring at me. Why can't I move my limbs? Why is my head so numb? Maybe I'll die here, rooted to the floor, and they'll bronze me as a monument to the unknown student."

Take heart—it doesn't have to be like this. Let me give you the first step so that you be free from bondage. It's simple—*Get a working knowledge of your topic.*

Right, so what's a working knowledge? Here's a basic definition: *You have a working knowledge of a topic when you can talk about it for one minute without repeating yourself.*

To start research, all you need to do is acquire one minute's knowledge. "One minute?" you say. "I've been told I have to present a fifteen page research paper with a dozen footnotes including appropriate periodical literature (whatever that is). Why talk to me about one minute of working knowledge?"

I'm introducing you to a working knowledge for the same reason that you take a flashlight with you when you have to stumble around in the dark. A working knowledge gives you the basics of a topic, enough light so that you won't hurt yourself as you move on into heavier materials. It isn't complete knowledge, but it's enough to tell you what the topic entails, what its boundaries are, even what some of its controversies and mysteries might be.

So where do you get a working knowledge? From *reference sources.* All academic libraries, and even many sites on the Internet, have reference tools that provide short, concise and authoritative information on virtually any topic you might think of.

Reference books will generally appear in the form of dictionaries or encyclopedias on general or specific topics. As well, handbooks, atlases— in fact, any tool that involves looking up brief information—may be found in a reference collection. Increasingly, reference sources are also appearing in computer form, allowing for greater flexibility in searching.

> So you're wondering how to find a reference book that will give you Information on marriage customs of the Kurdish people. You could wander the shelves of the reference collection, but there's an easier way to find what you want. *Think of the broad subject within which you topic lies.* In this case, you are looking at customs of a particular culture. Thus you could look up in your library's catalogue a subject heading like MANNERS AND CUSTOMS—ENCYCLOPE-DIAS to find a reference Source like *Worldmark Encyclopedia of Cultures and Daily Life.* Then just look up "Kurds."

Let's try an example. You've been dying to find out who the Lollards were (or are), admit it. Let me give you a clue—they were a group of religious people who flourished in the late middle ages and early reformation period. What sort of a reference source would you use for Lollards? How about a dictionary of church history? I check a couple of such dictionaries and, following the famous 5 W's of inquiry, I discover the following:

Who?

The Lollards were followers of John Wycliffe; more generally, the term was used of any serious critic of the church. Key figures in the movement were Nicholas of Hereford, William Swinderby, and John Purvey.

What?

Their teachings, summed up by the Twelve Conclusions of 1395, included personal faith, divine election, and the Bible as the sole authority in religion. They demanded that every person have the individual right to read and interpret the Bible.

Where?

The movement existed primarily in England and Scotland.

When?

It began in the 1380s (AD) and went underground after 1431 due to persecution. It declined in the mid-1400s but revived about 1490. It figured prominently in the congregational dissent of the seventeenth century and the rise of the Hussites in Bohemia.

Why?

The Lollards claimed to be a reaction to the control over human life and spirituality exercised by the Church of the time.

My two reference sources (*Oxford Dictionary of the Christian Church* and *New International Dictionary of the Christian Church*) also yielded a combined bibliography of over 15 sources on the Lollards.

Have I convinced you of the need for a working knowledge? If not, I hope you have lots of luck in your research—You're going to need it. Unless you start with a working knowledge you will inevitably flounder when you reach deeper waters.

Finding a Good Question

Research is not research until you have focused it around a solid research question. But how do you come up with a question that is going to work?

1. **Narrow your Topic** to one aspect of it. One of the biggest reasons why research fails is that the researcher is trying to conquer the world with one project. You simply cannot cover all of the topic of teen suicide or abortion or the causes of World War

One or how Martha Stewart can do what she does and still be only one person. You have to choose an aspect that is distinct enough that you can really work with it.

2. **Identify Controversies or Questions** related to your narrowed approach. There's no point re-describing what has already been described. To tell me once more who the Lollards were is to do what every reference source on the subject has already done. This is where those excruciatingly boring and superficial "research" papers come from. You must vow never to write another one. Find something worth investigating. In the case of the Lollards, you might want to focus on one of them (narrowing) such as Nicholas of Hereford, and discover what elements of his approach were effective putting forward his Lollard position (the research question).

> Remember one crucial thing, however: *You must never use more than one research question per research project.* The shotgun approach is out. Research identifies *one* question, deals with that question through analytical use of data, and *then quits.* Never *ever* get stuck in the kind of proposal that says, "This paper will deal with _____. I will also attempt to _____ and to _____ and to _____." Your second and third questions are loose torpedoes on your own ship. They will sink you because they'll kill your focus. One question per research project is all you need or want.

How About a Few Examples?

"The Thought of Erasmus of Rotterdam"
Your much beloved philosophy professor has assigned you "The Thought of Erasmus of Rotterdam." Having studied a few philosophy dictionaries, you narrow your topic to "The Humanism of Erasmus of Rotterdam." You *could*, at this point, decide to begin your paper with "Erasmus of Rotterdam was born in the year…" You *could* go on to explain what he taught about humanism and then conclude, "It is clear that Erasmus was an important person who deserves more attention.

This method is also called "regurgitating your sources." It establishes a conduit between your books and your writing hand without ever really engaging your brain. It also makes for a very dull paper. Professors fall asleep over dull papers.

On the other hand, you could be analytical. Having read your sources and affixed your working knowledge firmly in your mind, you could engage your brain in finding a research question. How about asking this: "What is the essential difference between the humanism of Erasmus and that of the modern *Humanist Manifestos I and II*?" This would certainly demand study of Erasmus, but it would go further.

Now your have the makings of an approach that could contribute something fresh and exciting to the topic.

~~~~~~~~~~~~~~~~~~~~~~~~~~~~~~~~

"Homelessness in our Cities"
You are taking a sociology class and are supposed to write a paper on "Homelessness in our Cities." You could regurgitate some statistics, recite a few case studies and conclude, "It is obvious that we need to take action on this issue." Or you might narrow your topic and ask a research question like this one: "Do programs that arrest homeless teens and compel them to accept social worker assistance actually reduce incidence teen of homelessness in the long run?"

~~~~~~~~~~~~~~~~~~~~~~~~~~~~~~~~

"The Causes of the Ecological Crisis"
For a course on environmental issues, you have been assigned, "The Causes of the Ecological Crisis." You narrow this to focus on human values in society that can lead to ecological problems.

A descriptive paper would string together quotations from current leaders in the debate who are decrying our attitudes of wastefulness and greed. Your conclusion could read, "Thus it is clear that we must change our attitudes." You have narrowed your topic, but you've failed to apply a research question to it.

An analytical research paper would go further, perhaps considering the common view that the western Protestant ethic, with its desire for dominion over the earth is at the heart of the environmental trouble we are in. Your research question could be, "Is western Protestantism responsible for the environmental crisis?"

~~~~~~~~~~~~~~~~~~~~~~~~~~~~~~~~

> **"Behaviorism as a Model for Social Engineering"**
> You have been given a topic which is fairly narrow but still covers a lot of territory. Why not narrow it down to the behavioristic model of B.F. Skinner? You might now take the easy way and summarize his book *Walden Two* as Skinner's model for social engineering (but easy is the way that leads to destruction).
>
> Or you could ask how Skinner's model in *Walden Two* might need to be revised if basic human depravity were taken into account (something Skinner seemed blissfully unaware of).

➤One final note of caution: *Always clear your narrowed-down topic and brilliant research question with your professor or supervisor.* Disaster could be awaiting you if you don't.

Of course, some of us **like** to flirt with disaster. Do you feel lucky?

2

Databases

There was a time when dinosaurs roamed the earth and every library had a card catalogue. Things were easier then. To find a book, you had one of three options—look up an author, look up a title, or look up a subject heading. Things may be much more complicated now, but your power to search has multiplied because of the computer.

The Next Stage

Once you have a working knowledge of your topic and a sound research question (only *one* research question, remember?), you need to move on to more substantial materials, most often to books in libraries. Why go there first rather than to magazines or journals or the Internet? For several reasons:

❖Books represent the established knowledge concerning a topic, while journal articles and Internet tend toward more experimental knowledge.
❖Books tend to cover the topic more comprehensively, while journal articles look at far more narrow aspects of the topic.

❖Books, as we will see in the next chapter, are dandy resources for further bibliography.

So how do you find books? One source of useful book titles has already made itself available to you—most reference book articles have at the end of them a bibliography of key works on the topic. Make use of this resource. Beyond that, you will need to search a library catalogue. These days, most often this means that you will be using a computer.

It would be great if I could present to you one version of a computerized library catalogue and say, "Learn how to use this, and you can do a search for books in any library in the world." But the fact is that there are dozens of different computer catalogue programs around, and each uses a different set of search techniques.

Far better, for your purposes, would be an explanation of databases and how they work. Armed with this information, you can face any threatening computer catalogue with courage and skill. So on to databases!

Database Searching

Why would anyone except a techno-genius want anything to do with a database? Doing a database search seems akin to asking a dentist to perform a root canal on a tooth that doesn't need it.

Actually, databases are everywhere, and I guarantee you've already searched one or more. When was the last time you used a phone book, a library catalogue (even in card format), a dictionary? All of these are databases. Here's a definition:

A database is any organized collection of data
that can be retrieved using organized search procedures.

Phone books are databases of names, addresses and phone numbers. They are *organized* alphabetically, and they use an *organized search procedure* involving the alphabet to help us retrieve the data we need. (NOTE: Just to confuse us, the Yellow Pages are organized by subject, then by alphabet).

Most common print databases are easy to search. But when those databases are in computerized form, a whole new set of problems emerges:

1.   Computer databases are generally much larger than print ones.
2.   There are few common conventions for organizing and searching computerized databases, so every new database is a new experience.
3.   Unlike a phone book or a library catalogue in card format, you can't really browse a database well. It's like a black hole into which you are calling: "Please send me the information I want!" Computers, being inherently unintelligent, don't always understand what you want, and thus frustration sets in quickly.

Many people today are hotshots on computers. They can make the keys sing, the mouse roar and the CPU toast. But not many people today understand database searching well enough to do it efficiently.

Case in point-I recently found the dregs of a search on a computerized periodical index database. The database itself has over 1,000,000 journal article citations listed in it, and this searcher had typed in the keyword *Johnson*, resulting in 4,386 hits. That is, 4,386 journal citations with the name *Johnson* had become available to him/her. What was worse, the searcher had actually started pulling up each of those 4,386 entries in turn, looking for the right one. Ten hours later, red-eyed, fingers like angry claws…one can only imagine the angst that this session built up.

You may know how to use a computer, but disaster will befall you if you don't understand databases. Fear not, however. You are about to learn a few things.

The big problem with computer databases is not with getting information into them, but with *retrieving* the information you need. For this purpose, there are two basic search tools available to you: *controlled vocabularies* and *keywords*. Let's look at each in turn.

Controlled Vocabularies

They sound nasty, but you're actually quite familiar with them already if you've done much work in a library. The most common controlled vocabulary system in all of North America is the *Library of Congress Subject Headings* system, used in most libraries. Let's take that as a model.

How did subject headings originate? Quite simply, the Library of Congress (LC) in Washington, DC predetermined the terms by which most things in the world would be called and then organized these terms in alphabetical lists. Some subject headings were easy: dogs are **DOGS**, sunflowers are **SUNFLOWERS**, and so on. Some were more difficult: What do you call senior citizens? LC chose **AGED**, much to the outrage of senior citizens. Television faith healers are **HEALERS IN MASS MEDIA**. Why? *Because LC said so.* That's the point with controlled vocabularies. These vocabularies are created by people "out there" who then *control* them. Thus:

Rule #1: With controlled vocabularies, you have to use the subject terms provided by the system. No options are allowed.

How does a controlled vocabulary work? Armed with a set of subject headings, cataloguers assign subject headings to chunks of data. In the case of LC, every time they get a book to catalogue, they write a description of the book (i.e. the catalogue entry) which then becomes data, and to that data is added one or more controlled subject headings. So a book entitled *Them TV Preachers* may have the subject heading **HEALERS IN MASS MEDIA** attached to it. A book called *Active Seniors in Today's World* may be labeled with the subject heading **AGED**.

Note something very important here. The book *Them TV Preachers* did not have any of the actual words of the subject heading in its title. The title said nothing about healers or about mass media. The same was true for the second title—*Active Seniors in Today's World*—the term "aged" is not to be seen anywhere in the title. Why were they given the subject headings they received? *Because some intelligent librarian sat down with these books, determined what they were about, and then assigned the closest subject headings from the already existing controlled vocabulary list.* Thus:

> *Rule #2: The actual wording of the data record (book title or catalogue entry) is not important for controlled vocabularies. Subject headings are assigned on the basis of somebody's judgment as to what the data is about.*

Consider the advantages: I have 5 books with the following titles:

Terminal Choices	*Choosing Life or Death*
Euthanasia	*The Practice of Death*
The Right to Die	

All of them are about mercy killing or euthanasia. You might not have guessed that fact by looking at the titles, but the intelligent LC librarian has looked over these books determined that they are all about the same topic and assigned them all the same subject heading:

EUTHANASIA.

Controlled vocabularies are a good solution to the difficulty that when we are presented with a database to search, our main problem is *retrieval.* How do we ask the right question so that the database will deliver to us the information we need? If we want a list of books about euthanasia, it would be nice to have a search tool that would enable us simply to type a word or phrase into the computer and get back a euthanasia book list regardless of the wordings of the actual book titles. This is what a *controlled vocabulary* is designed for . Most of the books on euthanasia in a library will be retrieved just by typing in the subject term **EUTHANASIA**.

> *Rule #3: Use a controlled vocabulary as a search tool when you want a collection of data on the same subject regardless of what the data actually says about itself.*

Just before we leave *LC Subject Headings,* let's see how this controlled vocabulary system works. The Library of Congress uses its subject headings for its own books, but it has also conveniently issued its list of approved headings so that all of us can use their system. Most libraries in North America have chosen to do just that, so that your library's subject headings are likely derived from the Library of Congress.

Your library should have an edition of the LC subject headings guide in the form of a set of large red volumes or a microfiche edition or even a computerized version. Below is a typical page from the guide. On the right is what you will see on a typical page. On the left is a description of what you are seeing. If you have trouble distinguishing left from right, look for italics (left) or non-italics (right):

LC authorized subject heading (bold print)-> **Peanuts**
　　　　　　　　　　　　　　　　[QK495.L52
(Botany)]
Library of Congress Class numbers for peanuts-> [SB351.P3
(Culture)]
　　　　　　　　　　　　　　UF Arachides
UF = "use for". These are terms　Arachis hypogea
which LC does not use or authorize.　　Earth nuts
If you looked up "Earth nuts" in LC　　Goobers
Subject Headings, *it would say*:　　Grass nuts
USE Peanuts.　　　　　　　　Ground-nuts
　　　　　　　　　　　　　　Groundnuts
(Bet you never knew peanuts could　Monkey nuts
called so many things. "Goobers?")　Pindars
　　　　　　　　　　　　　　Pindas
　　　　　　　　　　　　　　Pinders
BT = "broader term." Peanuts　　BT Arachis
are a subdivision of these.　　　Oilseed plants
RT = "related term"　　　　RT Cookery (Peanuts)
NT = "narrower term"　　　NT Peanut products
　　　　　　　　　　　　　　—Breeding
These are subdivisions of　　　—Irrigation
"peanuts." There's even one　　—Law and legislation
subdivision of a subdivision:　　—Storage
Peanuts — Storage — Diseases　--Diseases and injuries
and injuries.

Here are other types of computer databases in which you may find controlled vocabularies:

1. Some periodical indexes (see chapter 4 for definition)-A number of indexes offer the possibility of a "subject heading" or "subject alphabetical" search. Beware, however: the subject heading terms may not be the same as those used by LC. To offer some assistance, you may find a printed *Thesaurus* near the computer terminal. This is a subject heading list for that particular index. Or the computer may have a "browse" function that allows you to type in what you think the subject heading is. The browser will take you to the place in the computer's internal alphabetical subject heading list that is closest to what you asked for, and you can see whether or not you were right.

2. The ERIC database (see chapter 5 for explanation)-This database (available on the Internet at **http://ericir.sunsite.syr.edu**) offers the possibility of searching by keyword or by "descriptor." A descriptor is a controlled vocabulary term. ERIC suggests that to find out what descriptors they use you should consult their printed *Thesaurus* or search for some documents by keyword, then note down some of the descriptors used with the data you recover. After that, you can search by those descriptor terms.

Many databases today, including most of those on the Internet, can be searched only by keyword. As we will see, keywords have distinct advantages, but the lack of a controlled vocabulary search option can be a definite drawback when all you want is a set of data on one subject regardless of what the data says about itself.

Keywords

Controlled vocabularies are subject terms created and administered by real human beings. That's civilization. Keywords represent the Wild West of database searching-bold and exciting, but risky as can be.

Every database is made up of words. Computers, though inherently unintelligent when it comes to real thinking, are experts at recognizing words. To understand how keyword searching works, imagine the old card catalogue days. Back then, when a book was catalogued by a library, a *record* or card catalogue entry was created. It might look something like this:

HF5386	Tucker, Robert B., 1953-
.T828	Managing the future : 10 driving
1991	forces of change for the '90's / Robert
	B. Tucker.—New York : Putnam, c1991.
	233 p. ; 23 cm.
	Includes bibliographical references
	(p. 219-225) and index.
	ISBN 0-399-13576-6 (alk. Paper)
	1. Success in business. 2.
	Management. 3. Competition. I. Title.

In that one *record* is all the data which the cataloguer has provided about that book. If the record now is put into computerized form, the computer should be able to search for *any word* in that record. Now, imagine that there are thousands of records, and I'm interested in finding a list of books about the management of companies in the future. I should be able to think of important words (= *keywords*) and input them as a computer search. The computer will then look for those words in each of the records in the database and will download to my screen any records that have the words I've asked for. In this case, my search might look like this:

```
manag* and future
```

(Don't worry about the search form yet. We'll get to the details in the box just below).
I will get records for books with titles like:
A Manager's Look at the Future

The Future of Management
Is There a Future for Today's Manager?

Notice one little trick I performed—*TRUNCATION* (sometimes called *WILDCARDS*). In many keyword searches, you can type part of a word, then add an asterisk (*) or sometimes a question mark (?), and the computer will look for every word that begins with the letters you typed. E.g. **manag*** will ask the computer to search for **manage, managing, management, manager, manages, managers, managerial** and so on.

You can also sometimes do **forward truncation** in which the asterisk goes at the beginning (rare) or **middle,** in which truncation is done in the middle of a word (e.g. Wom*n)

Even given the variations allowed through truncation, you need to admit that keyword searching demands just as much precision as controlled vocabulary searching. The computer will only find the exact thing you want it to find. If you mistakenly type **mang*** instead of **manag***, the computer will give you data with the words **mange** or **mangle** in it.

Rule #1: With keyword searching, what you type is what you get. The computer cannot interpret your request or give you the next best solution. All it can do is identify the words you ask for and give you the related data.

Boolean Searching

Many years before computers, a man named George Boole invented a system of algebra that enabled people to visualize the combination of various classes of things. The computer people have taken his system into the world of database searching in order to formulate searches where two or more terms are used. Let's look at some of the basic commands used:

The "OR" Command

Suppose that I'm looking in a database for information about cars. I realize that a keyword search will pull out all information that has the word "cars" in it, but some people use the term "automobiles." How can I tell the computer to look for *both* words at the same time and give me data whether that data uses the word "cars" *or* the word "automobiles?"

In a situation in which I am searching for synonyms-different words that mean the same thing-I use the "OR" command. Let's visualize it this way:

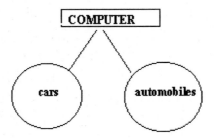

That is, "Computer, please give me everything on cars or automobiles, I don't care which. So you will get all the data with "cars" in it, plus all the data with "automobiles" in it.

In a keyword search in a computer catalogue or some other database, your search may look like this:

> cars or automobiles

Another situation calling for an **"or"** search might be that in which two concepts are closely related, and you suspect that finding data on either of them will further your overall goal. For example, in doing a search for "psychoanalysis" you might be well advised to search as well for the father of psychoanalysis-Sigmund Freud. If you leave off the "Sigmund" (because he is often referred to just as "Freud"), you can formulate a search like this:

psychoanalysis or Freud

With an **"or"** search, you typically get a lot of "hits", that is, pieces of data brought down to you out of the database.

Rule #2: An "or" search is usually for synonyms or for keywords that are already closely related. With it, you are trying to anticipate the various ways something might be described or approached.

The "AND" Command

One of the most profitable uses of keywords is in combining topics to narrow down a search. For example, a *Library of Congress Subject Heading* might lead you to something fairly narrow like "**Mental Health—Religious Aspects.**" But what if you wanted to look at information on the relationship between prayer and mental health? A subject heading search will probably let you down, *but a keyword search is just the ticket.*

Let's visualize it with a diagram first. If you're searching for the relationship between prayer and mental health, you don't want every piece of data on mental health, nor do you want every piece of data about prayer. You want the data that comes from having mental health and prayer intersect. Thus:

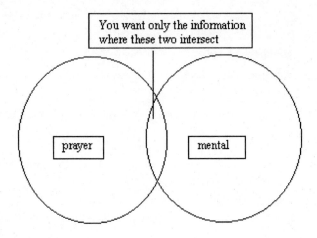

Your formulated keyword search will look like this:

> **prayer and mental**

What about the word "health?" The genius of keyword searching is that you can often cover most of your bases without inputting all the words you would normally use in a controlled vocabulary subject heading. In this case, I've made the judgment call to omit the word "health" from the search, assuming that "mental" will most often refer either to mental health or mental illness. If you wanted to include "health", your search would be:

> **prayer and mental and health**

Now, suppose that you wanted to complicate things a bit by looking at the relationship between prayer and mental health or mental illness. You could formulate a search combining and with or:

> **prayer and mental and (health or illness)**

Notice that you are still demanding that the data have both the word **prayer** and the word **mental** in it. In addition, the data must have either the word **health** or the word **illness** in it. By putting parentheses around **health or illness,** you avoid confusing the computer. You're telling it that your *"and"* search has an *"or"* search within it.

Rule #3: **A keyword "and" search is used to search for data that relates two topics or concepts together. The data found will show the effect of the relationship of these topics.**

An **"and"** search is a limiting kind of search. It asks the computer to give data only when that data contains *both* keywords. Thus, you should expect that an **"and"** search will give you fewer hits than if you had searched each keyword on its own. This is a difficult concept for many people to grasp. If you're having trouble with it, go back up to the **"and"** search diagram above. Or consider the example above: you don't want every piece of data about prayer or every piece of data about mental health. You want only the data that relates mental health and prayer. Thus the **"and"** search has set limits for your search. It has narrowed down the data that you want to receive.

Rule #4: **"And" searches will narrow or limit your topic. Thus you can expect that you will not get as many "hits" with an "and" search as with an "or" search.**

With the **"and"** search, as well, you need to recognize that adding more **"ands"** simply guarantees fewer hits. Outside of **"or"** searching, you will find, as a whole, that putting more keywords on the screen leads to fewer results. For example, if I formulate this search:

> prayer and mental and health and Canada and twentieth and century

I can expect few if any hits. What I've told the computer is that I only want data if it is about the relationship between prayer and mental health in Canada in the twentieth century. I've put pressure on the computer that's probably left it muttering to itself in frustration. It's a sure thing that a cheesed-off computer is not going to go out of its way to help me.

The "Not" Command

You're back to looking for information about cars, but the one type of car you're *not* interested in is any car made in Europe (I don't want to get cards and letters asking why I have a problem with European cars-It's a long story). You wish you could tell the computer to give your everything about cars but not give you any data about European cars. Here's how to do a **"not"** search:

> (cars or automobiles) not Europe*

Notice what I've done. First, I remembered that "automobiles" is a synonym for "cars." Thus I included both, putting them in parentheses so as not to confuse the computer as to what I meant by my **"not"** command. Then I added the **"not"** and did a truncation on Europe (using an asterisk) so the computer could look for "Europe" and "European" with a single search. What I'm saying is that I want data about either cars or automobiles as long as it doesn't refer to European cars or automobiles.

Exceptions to the Above

Exceptions? Why are there always exceptions? Probably because every database likes to do its own thing. Here are some variations that you may find to the standard Boolean or, and, not searches:

❖ Some databases want you to put your linking words in capital letters-OR AND NOT

❖ In many databases, you can do an "and" search simply by leaving a space between words. Instead of:

> **prayer and mental**

you can type:

> **prayer mental**

But note that some other databases will see "prayer mental" as a phrase where the two words have to be found together in that order.

❖ Internet keyword searches often use + and-signs. Thus

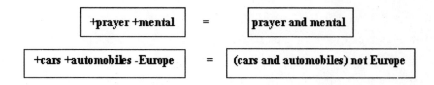

| **+prayer +mental** | = | **prayer and mental** |
| **+cars +automobiles -Europe** | = | **(cars and automobiles) not Europe** |

With these kinds of searches, if you just leave a space between keywords, you are asking for an **"and"** search, but only until there is no further data that uses the words in combination. Then the search engine searches for at least one of the terms (=an **"or"** search).

❖ In some databases, **"not"** has to be expressed as **"and not"**.

❖ Some databases ask you to put quotation marks around words that need to appear together, e.g.:

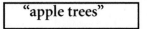

❖ There are some databases now that actually search for synonyms of the term(s) you input so that they can bring up material you might not have found through a simple keyword search.

❖ Some databases provide a choice of buttons under the search box, like this:

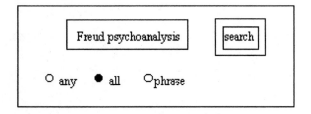

Complex Keyword Searches

Many databases now allow you to build your own search. They do this through a grid arrangement that allows you to specify *what type of words in what types of combinations you want to search*. Don't worry, it's not nearly as horrifying as it looks. Let's consider an example, remembering that the look and features of these search grid formats vary depending on what database you're searching.

The top part of the grid will look like this.

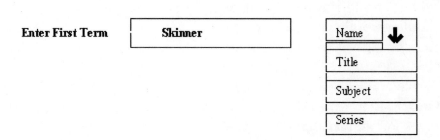

Note that you can click your mouse button on the downward arrow to open up a table of possible typed of words you can search for. If you click on the one you want, it will appear in the search box.

Now let's look at an actual complex keyword search with the whole grid present:

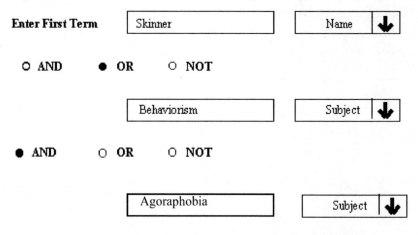

Let's decipher the above search. I am asking for the name *Skinner* or the subject heading *Behaviorism* as long as either term is also associated with *agoraphobia* (the fear of going out into crowds). In other words, I want to know what Skinner (a behaviorist) or the therapy of Behaviorism have to say about Agoraphobia.

Notice how the boundaries between keywords and controlled vocabularies are blurring here. I am linking a keyword name with two subject heading words. At the same time, this remains a keyword search because it is linking words using Boolean search strategies.

Natural Language Searching

Natural language searching is a variation on the standard keyword search. It tries to imitate the way you would ask another person a question. Rather than inputting a few important words in a certain combination, it lets you simply ask a question, for example:

"What was the name of the Lone Ranger's Horse?"

Computers are not intelligent. They don't actually see a formulated question when they look at the sentence above. Rather, a natural language program picks up on key words-"name," "Lone," "Ranger's" "Horse"-and formulates an "and" search for you. A few databases and even some Internet search engines are playing around with natural language searches. For your part, you're probably better off learning and using Boolean functions, which tend to be more precise.

Some Final Hints

❖ Before you begin a search, you need to think: "What is this topic about? What are the important words that define it?" That is, you need to *label* your topic with its favorite jargon.

❖ Consider whether or not you are connecting two or more concepts in unusual ways in dealing with your topic (e.g. Behaviorism and agoraphobia). If you are, controlled vocabularies will probably not work as effectively as keyword searches.

❖ Discover the narrowest possible terminology to describe your topic. If you are dealing with *Martin Luther,* don't search for *Church History.* If you want information on *homelessness,* don't search for *social problems.* Be as specific as you can in determining exactly what you need. If your database search turns up any more than about 100 "hits," you probably need to find more specific terminology. I can't believe how many times I've seen students working through 500 or more hits, **one at a time!** Can there be anything more numbing to the mind, damaging to the eyes, and carpal tunneling to the wrists?

❖   If you are doing a keyword **"and"** search, or a complex keyword search using a grid, remember that the more information you put on the screen, the fewer hits you will get.

❖   In most cases, believe it or not, controlled vocabularies will get you more and better results than will keyword searches. Keywords may be hot right now, but they are ultimately quick and dirty in their results. If you don't believe me, then why do most Internet keyword searches net thousands of results per search?

❖   Database searching is supposed to be *FUN*. If you're experiencing some other emotion, read this chapter again, cheer up, swallow your fear or boredom, and get out there searching.

3

Blowing Away the Information Fog

-Information hierarchies, library catalogues and bibliographies

Be honest. Do you really want to do this? Do you really want to learn how to be a researcher? We need to face the fact that research is tough. For most people it's only slightly less painful than being flogged with barbed wire. A big part of the problem, I've found, is that many beginning researchers have no idea where they are, and if they finally arrive, they can't tell you where they've been.

Research, for many of us, is like driving through a fog. You know a concrete world exists all around you, but you can't feel it or see it. The signposts are obscured, and even if you find your destination, you have no idea how you got there. A lot of research is like that-trial and error based on confusion. No wonder it's so painful.

A better analogy for proper research is the method a player uses in beating a video game. At each level, you use strategies intended to move you on to the next level. Once you've been playing for awhile, you have a keen sense of where you are going and what it will take to get there. As each level is conquered, you move closer to that magic moment when you've beaten the whole game.

So how do we blow away the fog and start playing the game in earnest? Actually, some of the most important strategies are already part of your arsenal-Getting a working knowledge of your topic, developing a research question, putting together a preliminary outline, beginning to search the library catalogue. So let's move on

Finding your Way in an Information Hierarchy

If you want the fog really to be gone, you're going to have to learn some theory about the way information is structured. Theory? No way! This is supposed to be a practical book about getting research done efficiently and (hopefully) in a hurry. Theory will only get in the way.

Before you give up that quickly, let's see what theory can do for you. Here's a question: Can you define the following word?

ROCK

"Sure," you say. "It's a hard object that comes out of the ground."

To which I answer, "How wrong you are! Don't you know that 'rock' is a verb? My definition, a symptom my growing age, is that the only rock worth anything is the rock I do in my rocking chair.

"I'm not wrong," you retort. "You're wrong."

To which your friend standing next to us says with a smirk, "You're both wrong. Rock is a kind of music, and I'd rather be listening to it than hearing you argue about such an inane subject."

What's the problem here? Why can't we agree on a definition for one word with only four letters in it?

The reason is simple:

> Words by themselves don't really mean anything for certain. They only have a definite meaning when you put them in a context.

Words by themselves don't really mean anything for certain. They only have a definite meaning when you put them in a context.

If I say, "I'm planning to take a whole evening to rock in my rocking chair," you know that my definition of 'rock' is something like 'a rolling back and forth motion.' If, on the other hand, I say, "The rock that went through my window was two inches across," you know that 'rock' is now a noun meaning 'a hard substance taken from the earth.'

Words get their meaning from the sentences surrounding them. In turn, sentences become understandable within their paragraphs and paragraphs make sense within the larger context of the complete document. The important word here is "context." Meaning is derived from context, and without context we have only confusion.

So what? How do meaning and context relate to research? Like this:

> All data comes within a context. Without context the data cannot tell us what we need to know.

If you want to get technical, all data exists within one or more information hierarchies. Let me illustrate with the word "rock."

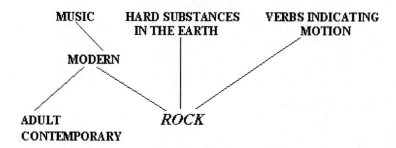

"Rock' is sub-class of something more comprehensive. For example, "rock" may be a sub-class of modern music, right alongside other sub-classes like "adult contemporary," "elevator music," and the compositions of John Cage. "Modern music" in turn is a sub-class of the larger category of "music" along with other sub-classes like "classical," "baroque," etc. What we end up with is a hierarchy. Each higher grouping is more general than the one below it.

But notice that "rock" is capable of having several different hierarchies attached to it , depending on the meaning we give to the word. It can also be a sub-class of "hard substances from the earth" or of "verbs indicating motion."

Let's now move into an area that better resembles a research topic. Take something like the Roman emperor Constantine. Depending on how you approach him, he can exist within a number of contexts (= hierarchies):

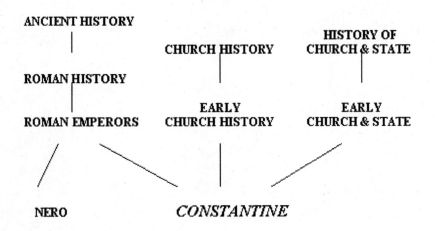

You can deal with him as a sub-class of "Roman emperors" alongside other sub-classes like Julius Caesar and Nero. "Roman emperors" in turn are a sub-class of "Roman history", which in turn is a sub-class of "Ancient History."

Alternatively, you can deal with him as an important figure within the larger subject of "Early Christian Church History," since he was the emperor who declared Christianity the official religion of his empire.

Or you can discuss him within the higher class of "History of Church and State," since his creation of a marriage between empire and Christianity led to many issues related to the wisdom of creating such unions.

Each of these hierarchies leads to a different approach to the same topic.

All information is hierarchical. The rule is simply this:

In research, you must always know where you are in the hierarchy.

What higher class does your topic belong to? What exists above that class? Are there other hierarchies your topic could belong to? Are there sub-classes of your topic which could become factors to consider?

Take "homelessness." This topic might belong to a higher class of the "sociology of cities" (since most of the homeless seem to live in cities). "Sociology of cities" in turn is a sub-class of "sociology." But "homelessness" could exist within other hierarchies, e.g. "government policy toward the poor," or "issues of housing in modern society," or "current issues in social work." In turn, "homelessness" could have sub-classes such as "How do people become homeless?" or "What do we do about the minority of the homeless who don't want a home to live in?" or "How do we educate homeless children?"

This is how we would diagram it:

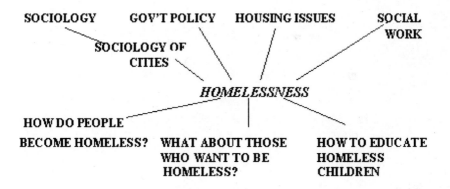

The reason for all this discussion of hierarchies is simply this:

If you know where you are, you can find your way to where you should be.

Let me show you how this could work with the topic of "homelessness:" Once I have identified the issues related to the topic and developed a working knowledge, I choose to deal with the issue of providing an education to children in homeless families, particularly families which are in and out of temporary shelters set up for people without homes. Now I need to ask myself, "Who would be interested in working with such children?" Obviously the educational system wants to educate them, but it is doubtful that school boards themselves search out such children. Thus, this topic, while educational in nature, is likely not directly in the hierarchy:

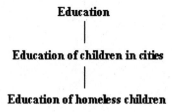

Education

|

Education of children in cities

|

Education of homeless children

Rather, it will probably be social workers involved with such families who will work to make sure that such children are put into an educational setting. Thus the hierarchy we are looking for is something like this:

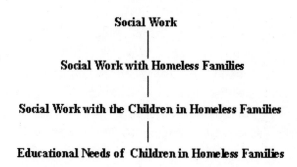

Social Work

|

Social Work with Homeless Families

|

Social Work with the Children in Homeless Families

|

Educational Needs of Children in Homeless Families

Once I have identified the discipline within which the subject is best treated, I have some idea where to go. What I may have to look for are Social Work policy statements on the issue, books on the social needs of homeless children, perhaps even interviews with people involved in working with children in this situation.

Let's look at another topic. You are in an ethics class and you need to do a research paper on "abortion." It sounds simple on the surface (which should have been your first clue to run for the hills). But you quickly find yourself bogged down in tons of detail and zillions of issues. You could, I suppose, simply chronicle the history and major issues of the abortion debate, but your paper will be a superficial regurgitation of your sources, nothing more. You need a *focus*.

This is the time to begin brainstorming possible hierarchies within which abortion could be discussed:

Philosophy : How do we define personhood? Is a fetus a person? If abortion is a matter of the relative values placed on completing a pregnancy as opposed to allowing women freedom with their own bodies, what values are being communicated?

Ethics: Should human beings maintain the right to continue or terminate a pregnancy? Is it true that advocating the right to abort a fetus is a "slippery slope" leading to euthanasia of the disabled and elderly?

Psychology: Is it true that an unwanted child can bring psychological harm to itself or its mother by being allowed to be born? Are the psychological after-effects of abortion in harmful to a woman's future well-being?

Law: Does the allowing of partial term abortions fit properly with other laws of the land? How well do existing abortion laws protect the rights of all concerned? Can abortion laws protect the rights of prospective fathers when their wishes are opposed to the wishes of prospective mothers?

Religion: How do the Christian views of life relate to Muslim views with regard to abortion? How logical is the Evangelical Christian or Catholic argument against abortion?

Hierarchy is virtually everything when it comes to grappling seriously with a topic. You must ask yourself from the outset, **"What is this topic a part of?"** Once you can determine which hierarchy you want it to fit into, you can begin addressing it with focus.

Hierarchy can help in another way: If you can't find a book particularly on your topic, you may be able to find a book dealing with a higher level of the hierarchy. For example:

> If you can't find a book on Constantine, you might find a book on Roman Emperors or Roman History of his era or Early Church History.

> If you can't find a book on Abortion, you might find one on Medical Ethics

In a pinch, though it might sound goofy, you can do a spatial trick in a library that might help you a lot. Find the specific place in your library where your topic should be treated. If there aren't enough books to satisfy you, *move to the left.* Why? Because classification systems in libraries move to the right from the general to the specific. If you back up by moving to the left, you will move *up the hierarchy* to the more general discipline out of which your topic came. This doesn't always work, but it can be a helpful strategy when you're desperate.

Strategies to Clear the Fog in the Book Collection

Books tend to create fogs of misunderstanding, because they're blunt instruments. In order to write a book, you need a topic broad enough to be covered in a couple of hundred or more pages, but you need enough focus to avoid it becoming multi-volume or being superficial. Thus finding a book on your narrowed down topic that is driven by a research question may well be a challenge. Generally, you need to assume that few books will be exactly on your topic. That is why strategies are needed.

Making the Catalogue Work For You

1.   Choices, choices—keyword or controlled vocabulary?
If your topic is somewhat standard, you will probably do best with a controlled vocabulary subject heading search. It's safer in that you know you will find most books that are available on the topic. The only problem is that the chances are you will only need a portion of the information found in each book. For example, if your research question is, "What's right and wrong with B.F. Skinner's utopian vision in his book *Walden Two?*" you might well find that there are few

books available specifically on *Walden Two*, and you are going to have to do a controlled vocabulary subject search on **Skinner, B.F. (Burrhus Frederic), 1904**-and then study within books describing his thought to see what they say about *Walden Two*. You'll also, of course, have to look at *Walden Two* itself.

If your topic is not a standard one or if it combines a couple of subject disciples (such as the influence of *Walden Two* on the 1960's hippy movement), you may want to go for a keyword approach. Here are a few warnings, however:

❖   If you are working in a small library, keywords are less useful, since they tend to target specific and/or non-traditional approaches to topics. The library may not have enough diversity to meet your particular quirky need.

❖   Remember always that keyword searching, while it may narrow down your quest to exactly what you want, is a very inexact science. You have to have the right word(s) configured in the right way, and you are highly dependent on the actual terminology of titles in the collection.

❖   Be sure you don't use too many keywords at once. Start with one or two, and if that doesn't give you what you want, try one more. Rarely will you need more than three.

Above all in catalogue searching, use lateral thinking. What we have covered in information hierarchies, above, should help you if you ask yourself one or more of the following questions:

➤What hierarchy or hierarchies could this topic be a part of?
➤If I can't find a book specifically on my topic, what topic is next above it in the hierarchy?
➤If one approach is not working, what are other ways that I might look at the topic? (i.e. what other hierarchies could potentially contain the topic?)

Using Other People's Work Without Cheating —The Bibliography Search

Did you know that advanced scholars rarely do subject or keyword searches in catalogues? Before you assume that the problem is that advanced scholars are old and therefore have the same knowledge of a computer as a Neanderthal, let me assure you that this is not the case. Most advanced scholars know their way around computers pretty well. The reason they don't use catalogues very much is that they don't need to.

Imagine yourself as an advanced scholar. You've been working on your topic for years, maybe decades now. You regularly read just about anything of importance that's published. You know who your key fellow scholars are. If you want to continue keeping up with your field, how do you do it? By picking up a colleague's latest book or periodical article and reading it. Not only that, but you search out what your colleague is reading. Thus you pour over his/her bibliography and footnotes.

The reason why advanced scholars rarely do subject searches on their fields in library catalogues is that they are too busy reading the works and bibliographies of other scholars. This suggests another approach to searching for information on a topic—*making use of other people's bibliographies.* This is not theft or plagiarism—it's research.

Here's a strategy that could net you a whole host of materials:

➤Find a recent book on your topic. If there is no such thing in your library, find a recent reference book article with a bibliography, or a periodical article with footnotes.

➤Take note of the footnotes and/or bibliography and write down a citation for anything that looks relevant to your topic.

➤Here's the potentially tricky part, so light up a few more brain cells: Actually find some of the items you jotted down from the above step. (These may be books or periodical articles or whatever). Open them and study *their* footnotes and/or bibliographies.

➤Jot down any further items which interest you, locate them, and carry on the procedure until you wear yourself out.

Let's try an example:

I'm doing a paper on the British scholar C.S. Lewis. When I look up his name as a subject, I discover that the rather small library I am using has only three books on him, and two of these have been signed out. Is my problem simply that very little has been written about Lewis? It might help me to know the answer to that question before I trek twenty miles across town to another library. It would also be good to have an idea what are the standard titles on him before I go.

The one book I have located is David Barrett, *C.S. Lewis and His World* (1987). It's not even very new, though I suppose that for a topic like this even older works will be useful. In its bibliography I find listed the following titles:

> Humphrey Carpenter, *The Inklings* (1978)
> Jocelyn Gibb, ed. *Light on C.S. Lewis* (1965)
> R.I. Green and Walter Hooper, *C.S. Lewis: A Biography* (1974)
> John Peters, *C.S. Lewis: The Man and His Achievement* (1985)
> Chad Walsh, *The Literary Legacy of C.S. Lewis* (1979)

The day I make my journey across town to the other library, it's raining (inevitably). I take my soggy list and locate the book by John Peters, *C.S. Lewis: The Man and His Achievement*. It has no bibliography, but its endnotes reveal the following:

> Humphrey Carpenter, *The Inklings* (1978)
> Jocelyn Gibb, ed. *Light on C.S. Lewis* (1965)
> Carolyn Keefe, ed. *C.S. Lewis: Speaker and Teacher* (1971)
> W.L. White, *Images of Man in C.S. Lewis* (1970)

The first two of these titles were listed in the first book I searched, and here they are again. I decide to try to locate the book by Humphrey Carpenter, but Carpenter seems to be in hiding (maybe off building a cabinet). I do find *Light on C.S. Lewis* as well as *C.S. Lewis: Speaker and Teacher*. The latter gives me extensive information on Lewis' own works, particularly those which began as lectures. There are citations to reviews of these works as well.

My book bibliography search has paid off. Not only do I have more books, but I have data on some of Lewis' more obscure works, along with information on where to find reviews of them.

When you work with bibliographies, you can continue the process indefinitely, depending on how broad your library" resources are, how many items you need, and how exhausted you are beginning to feel. But eventually one of two things would happen:

❖ You may find that the bibliographies begin to refer to books that are very old and are thus either unavailable or irrelevant (depending on your subject). Notice that we see a rough progression in our searches above from newer to older materials.

❖ You may begin to see a lot of repeat citations. We have already found this with Carpenter, who seems to be on everybody's list. When you do see repeats, you know that you have likely discovered the most important works on the topic.

Why go through this kind of exercise at all? Looking at the titles of many of the items we found, we could say that most of them would be easily accessed by looking up, "LEWIS, C.S. (CLIVE STAPLES), 1898-1963 in the subject catalogue. This is true, and if you want just a few items on a topic the catalogue may serve your purposes well. But if you want more, there are three reasons why a book bibliography search could be helpful:

➤Bibliographies tend to reveal which works are considered to be the more important ones
➤It is entirely possible that some works you spot in a bibliography may be under a subject heading or classification number that you wouldn't have thought of using.
➤Bibliographies often contain treasures—works or parts of works you might not have discovered on your own.

Now that I've convinced you, hopefully, that this approach can help, you might be wondering why you should search the catalogue at all. Why not simply steal your bibliographies from other people? There are two good reasons not to make bibliography searching your exclusive method:

First, no writer is obligated to cite all the good books on a topic. Thus you may miss some very relevant material.

Second, authors can only cite those works available to them when they were writing. For more recent materials, you still need to use the library catalogue. For example, Kathryn Lindskoog's *The C.S. Lewis Hoax* (1988) might be useful, but you wouldn't have found it in the book bibliography search example above, because you began with a book published in 1987.

Thus you really need to use both methods. Depending on the topic, one may pay off more richly than the other, but both have their own contributions to make.

Using Subject Bibliographies

In some instances, careful people who love minute detail have produced whole volumes of bibliographies in specialized subject areas. If there is one for your subject, you may well have one of the best tools for finding more items on your topic. You can locate such a bibliography by looking up your subject area in the subject catalogue of your library by adding a sub-heading—"bibliography." Many libraries group their bibliographies in one area for quick access.

Subject bibliographies come in a variety of formats. The most useful provide a survey of the topic and then annotate (comment on) each bibliography entry, arranging entries under appropriate subdivisions of the subject.

A related form of good bibliography is the "research guide," which is either an annotated bibliography subdivided by subtopics, or a series of "bibliographical essays" which describe the subject area by referring to and describing key works in the field. The bibliographical essay can be very valuable to you because of the amount of description and evaluation it provides.

From this point, we leave the good and move into the bad and the ugly. Here we have the bibliography that is not subdivided or has no annotations. While it may be better than nothing, it can use up a lot of your valuable time while you try to find what you want. At least it will give you a splendid opportunity for growth and development (should you desire another one).

Take note, as well, of the fact that periodical articles often provide state-of-the-art subject bibliographies, citing the most current research. By the end of the next chapter, you will know how to locate such articles.

There is one drawback with most published subject bibliographies: They are dated. If a completed book manuscript takes six months to two years to be published, it is already somewhat out of date when it is released. By the time it has been sitting on the library shelf for five years, it's really becoming a fossil. Thus subject bibliographies are best used for picking up the standard works of the past.

In this chapter we have been looking primarily at ways to find book literature. We now move on to those challenging (and dreaded?) periodicals.

4

Making Your Way Through the Periodical Maze

Just when you thought that books were frightening enough, someone is sure to suggest to you that there's another whole world of research materials crying out for attention—periodicals. Periodicals? I'm referring to magazines, scholarly journals, annual publications, and so on.

Even thinking of using periodicals in a research project may produce in you a shudder of horror. You imagine sitting down in front of piles of journals, thumbing through each one in an anguished quest for something (anything!) on the "The Implications for Generation X of Max Weber's Approach to the Sociology of Cities." Hours later, in bitter defeat, you will emerge, red-eyed, with one article that is only vaguely relevant.

Periodical searching used to be done that way when your grandfather was a wee lad in school. Now things are very different, due to the rise of periodical indexes.

Before we get to that, let's work out what makes periodicals different from books. The two have many similarities: Often they are printed in the same format. Both have title pages and footnotes, etc. Both sit on shelves. Why then do they deserve separate chapters in a research book? For one simple reason—you can't catalogue a periodical like you catalogue a book.

When a librarian gets a new book for the collection, the book is catalogued and put on the shelf. After that, there is nothing to do but sign it out and check it back in until it falls apart. That cataloguer's job is done. But a journal title *keeps on arriving* every week or month or quarter or year. By definition, it is *periodical.* You can't catalogue it once and for all like you can a book, because it keeps changing as more issues are added to the growing collection.

While it might be possible for a librarian to assign a subject heading to each article in each periodical as it arrives and then to create a database in the catalogue so that you can find articles on any given topic, it just isn't practical. The book catalogue is designed for books, not for listing an ever increasing number of periodical articles.

Thus we have the periodical index.

What Periodical Indexes Are All About

Each year, a number of indexers sit down in front of piles of periodicals (usually all related to one subject discipline, such as psychology or history or religion) and enter data about each article into computers which eventually generate databases searchable by subject (or author or title or keyword, etc.).

The indexes that are produced are most often in computer form these days, though annual indexes in print form are still being produced in some disciplines. By doing a search, you can generate a list of articles from various periodicals that are relevant to the subject you are studying.

Before we go much farther, we need to distinguish two terms: *data* and *interface.*

Data is data. It's the material about a periodical article fed into the computer and, while it may grow, it never changes.

The *Interface* is what you actually see on the computer screen when you search for the data in a periodical index. It includes the screen display, search method, and so on. Interfaces change constantly. What this means is that the screen may look different the next time you use the index. The instructions on use may be different. Even the methods you need to use to search the index may be different. The data inside the computer is the same, but the means you use to extract it may be brand new. To deal with a new interface, do the following:

➢ *Read the instructions on the screen.* As well, look for anything that says "search tips" or "how to use this index," etc.

➢ Go back over the material in Chapter 2 on database searching. Does your new interface permit controlled vocabulary subject searching (clues will be reference to "subject headings" or to a "browse" function)? If you are to search by keywords, what sorts of Boolean terms are in use in this database?

➢ Try a search on a broad basis first, perhaps inputting only one keyword. If you get more than about 50 "hits" (listings of individual articles), look for a means to refine or narrow your search by adding more words.

Some Tips on Periodical Article Citations:

A periodical article citation is simply a description of a periodical article with sufficient information to help you find it. While the format of a citation may vary, this is the information usually provided:

Badke, William B. "Was Jesus a Disciple of John?" *Evangelical Quarterly* 62 (July 1990): 195-204.

First we have data on the author and title of the article itself. Then we are told what journal it is in. Then we have the volume number of the journal (usually a volume number is assigned for each new year of publication, so in our example, this is the 62nd year of publication). Then you have a date and page numbers where the article may be found.

A First Adventure with a Real Live Computerized Periodical Index

If you want to learn to swim in the shark-infested waters of periodical literature searching, you have to arm yourself and just jump in. Let's look at a sample search using the combined *Humanities and Social Science Index*. The interface you will see was developed for a network of academic institutions in British Columbia. For the same index in your own area, this interface may well be different, but you can still learn a few things from following the example below.

Enter search terms(s) and click on **Search** :

	in	Keyword ▼		Search	Browse

Started	Help		Quit	

Notice some of the features of this first screen

❖ There is a box that allows you to enter information
❖ While the term beside the box is "keyword," there is an arrow
   pointing downward, which gives you a clue that you can click on
   it to discover other types of terms that are searchable.
❖ There is a "search" key. Once you have entered your search
   terms, you can click your left mouse button on "search," and the
   computer should provide you with a list of articles on whatever
   you asked for.
❖ There is a "browse" function, which tells you that you may also
   be able to search for subject headings. At the very least, the
   browse function can tell you whether or not the keyword you
   entered is actually found in the database, and what related keywords are also there, since "browse" always leads you to an
   alphabetized list.
❖ There are some directions on how to formulate Boolean searches.
Let's move on to the next screen shot:

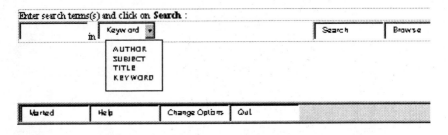

Clicking on "keyword" reveals that you can also search on title,
author or subject. I have highlighted "subject" as the search method I
want to use.

On to the next screen, where I have typed in a search term:

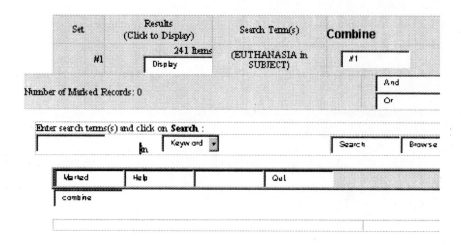

Having input the subject term "euthanasia," I am ready to click on the "search" button, resulting in the following:

At first the screen above looks like I haven't found anything, but wait—what's that number to the left under "results?" It says that there are 241 items on EUTHANASIA IN Subject. If I clicked on the "display" button, I would get a list of articles (though 241 of them are a bit too many to handle easily).

Sure enough—when I click on the results button in the bottom corner I see a citation to my first real live article. I discover that I can click on an item for a fuller display of the citation. I can also click to get the

next 15 records. As well, I can mark them so that I can hopefully download the citations I need or at least print them off.

Set #1: Search Results 1 to 15 of 241				
Search Term: (EUTHANASIA in SUBJECT)				
Next 15 records Jump to record:			Jump	
Marked	Print/Email	Return to Search	Help	Change Options

New search..adding search to cache

Mark	on	Holdings/Request Item	FullDisplay	record 1 of 241
	unchecked			

Ti: Dying made easy
Au: *McHugh, Paul R.*
So: Commentary , 107 no2, F '99, 13-17

Mark	on	Holdings/Request Item	FullDisplay	record 2 of 241
	unchecked			

Mark *Holdings/Request Item* record 2 of 241
Ti: The difference between Blacks' and whites' attitudes
           toward voluntary euthanasia etc.

Notice that the style in which the articles are cited is different from
the way you would find such articles listed in a bibliography in a

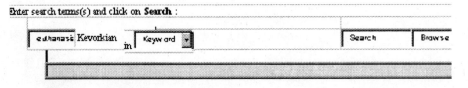

research paper. Formats for article citations in periodical indexes are as varied as the indexes themselves. The one thing they all have in com-

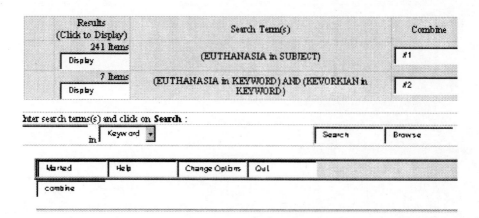

mon is that they provide sufficient information for you to be able to identify and hopefully locate the articles you need.

Let's now see if it's possible to narrow our search, so that we'll get fewer than 241 hits.

Set	Results (Click to Display)	Search Term(s)	Combine
#1	241 Items [Display]	(EUTHANASIA in SUBJECT)	#1

In order to narrow my topic, I decide to look for articles on euthanasia in relation to Jack

Kevorkian. I click on "Search" and:

Notice that I now have only 7 items—the "and" search narrowed down my results. If I click on the button that indicates my results, I should get a list of articles:

Set #2: Search Results 1 to 7 of 7

Search Term: (EUTHANASIA in *KEYWORD*) AND (KEVORKIAN in *KEYWORD*)

| Marked | PrinVEmail | Return to Search | Help | Change Options |

New search .. adding search to cache

| Mark | on | Holdings/Request Item | Full Display | record 1 of 7 |
| | unchecked |

Ti: Dying made easy
Au: McHugh, Paul R.
So: Commentary , 107 no2, F '99, 13-17

The first of these is displayed above, an article from a journal entitled
Commentary. Notice that you have all the information you need–title
and author of the article, journal title, volume, date and page numbers.

Remember the "browse" function we saw earlier?—of course you
don't, who could blame you? But this feature allows you to see a list of
words or headings so you can discover what's actually in the database and
how many articles are to be found related to your words or headings. In
this case, I type in "Kevorkian" as a *subject heading,* then click on browse:

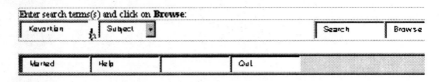

Enter search terms(s) and click on **Browse:**

| Kevorkian | Subject ▾ | | Search | Browse |

| Marked | Help | | Out |

A list emerges, and I can click on any heading to get the file of article
citations I want:

Mark	Term Found (Click to Search)
KEUREN	KEUREN
KEVN	KEVIN
KEVLAR	KEVLAR
KEVORKIAN	KEVORKIAN
KEVORKIAN-JAC	KEVORKIAN-JACK
KEW	KEW
KEWA	KEWA
KEWA-PAPUA-N	KEWA-PAPUA-NEW-GUINEA-PEOPLE
KEWA-PAPUA-N	KEWA-PAPUA-NEW-GUINEA-PEOPLE-FOLKLORE
KEWA-PAPUA-N	KEWA-PAPUA-NEW-GUINEA-PEOPLE-SOCIAL-LIFE-AND-CUSTOMS
KEWA-PAPUA-N	KEWA-PAPUA-NEW-GUINEA-PEOPLE-WOMEN
KEWEN	KEWEN

Search Marked 1 | Browse Back | Browse Forwan

Enter browse terms(s) and click on **Browse** :

Kevorkian in Subject ▼ | Browse

Click on any of the terms above, and you will get citations to related articles.

Tips and Hints

➤*Be prepared for frustration.* Periodical literature is not nearly as tidy as books are. You have a never-ending supply of them year after year after year, they can exist in a variety of formats (paper, microfilm, microfiche, computer files, Internet), and chances are the very article you need is nowhere to found in your metropolitan area.

Here's a psychological trick that might help you—*prepare yourself for frustration.* An illustration: If you are aware from long experience that you will face a traffic jam everyday on the way to work, you are ready for it. It's only if a traffic jam happens unexpectedly in a spot you didn't expect that it frustrates you. In the same way, if you prepare yourself for periodical index frustration, you're less likely the mutter to yourself when it happens. Before you start using an index, say to yourself, "I know this periodical search is going to tax the last fragments of my patience, but it's good for me, it really is, it really really is, and *I will succeed!"*

➢ *Resist the urge to fill the search screen with words.* Most keyword searches can be done with two words or, at the most, three. Remember this simple rule—the more you input into the search screen the more strain you're putting on your search. If it's an *and* search, you are telling the computer that you want *only* those articles that have every word you've entered (which often results in zero hits). If it's an *or* search, every article that has any one of your words will appear (resulting in thousands of hits sometimes). Get focused. Use as few words as you need to define your topic.

➢ *Think before you search.* Every new periodical index has a new interface, new search instructions, and so on. Even when you figure out how an index actually works, you need to think deeply about the terms you input. What will uniquely identify your topic in the minimum number of words? If your results show hit rates of 1,000 to 100,000 articles, you're probably aiming too broadly in your search, and you need to narrow down your terminology. If you are getting only one or two hits, you've probably gone too narrow by inputting too many search terms or asking for something so minute that there is only one scholar in the whole world who's remotely interested in the topic and she's on vacation.

➢ *Retrace your steps.* Be prepared to go back and figure out what you did wrong or how you could get better results. Look for buttons on the periodical index that allow you to "Refine Search" or "Search Again." Periodical index searching often demands experimentation to find just the right combination of terms that will nail down what you are looking for.

➢ *When in doubt, read the instructions.* Every periodical index worth its salt has instructions to guide you through the process of searching. When you've exhausted your own common sense, read the instructions. Different indexes have different capabilities and search techniques. You may find that the reason you get 354,000 hits one time and zero the next is that you are abusing the index by trying to make it do things it's not prepared to even contemplate.

➢ *Remain calm.* What's the most terrible thing that can happen if you blow a search? You might have to try again or (worst case scenario) one of your friends has watched you fail. Rarely will you have done any permanent harm to the index itself (unless you got violent, which is not recommended), so the only damage is to your time and your ego. If you find yourself hopelessly lost, there is usually a reference librarian to help you out. Swallow your pride and ask for help. Having a bad day in front of an index isn't the end of the world. Above all, resist those evil thoughts that take up residence in your mind, such as, "I will never ever get this" or, "For people like me, ignorant would be a step up" or, "I want to break something." Cool your heart and try again.

➢ *Sometimes problems arise because you're using the wrong index.* An index of agriculture journals won't help you with a psychology project. A history index won't be much good if you're researching cockroaches. Sometimes the problem may simply be that you're using a general index that covers many subjects and it doesn't cover enough journals in the specific

field you're dealing with. The right index for the right job is a
rule not to be forgotten.

Inside the New World of Periodical Indexes

The account of the history of periodical indexes used to be simple. It
went something like this: "In the beginning, there were no periodical
indexes. Then there were. You see those rows of volumes over there?
Those are the indexes. Go use them."

Now the world is a much more complicated place. In what follows, I
can only begin to acquaint you with the multitudes of changes occur-
ring in modern periodical indexes, and what I say today could well be
different tomorrow.

1.   The Shift from Print to Digital

Most periodical indexes, even in the 1980's were accessible only in
print format. Every year, a new volume of *History Index* or *Psychological
Abstracts* or *Book Review Index* would arrive at your local academic
library and be added to the volumes before it. If you wanted to search
for a subject, you found the appropriate index (by its subject discipline)
and then you started looking up your subject in volume after volume
until you had compiled a list of relevant articles. It was great to have
indexes available, but the tedium of searching, searching, searching
really got to people. Another problem was that the subject you were
searching for often crossed the boundaries of subject disciplines (e.g.
"The effect of eagle migration on work schedules of conservation offi-
cers"), so you often had no idea what subject to look up.

Computers have solved many of these problems. With a computer,
you should be able to input some search words *once* and search every
year of the computer index all at the same time. With a computer, you
should be able to combine keywords in new ways to narrow your search
to exactly what you want.

And so, today, most periodical indexes you encounter are going to be digital. You're going to need to sit in front of a computer screen and input search data. The advantages are tremendous—better searches in a shorter period of time, the ability to save your results to a file or to print them, even the potential of getting access to the full text of articles in digital form.

There are some downers, though:

➤ There are dozens and dozens of interfaces out there. Every computerized periodical index seems to have a search screen that looks different from every other one, and even searches differently. While there are some attempts being made to standardize interfaces, you may find that you have to get to know a lot of different ways of searching as you move from index to index. Look closely at the search screen before you start. Use the "help" or "search tips" button to get as much information as you need. If your results are bad, don't assume that the index is useless or there is nothing available on your topic—try another search with new techniques.

➤ Computers tend to be something of a black hole. You send in a request, and the computer index tells you what it found (or didn't find). The index will rarely tell you what you did wrong. It won't give you three 6.5's and an 8 like Olympic judges do. At least with the old print versions of computers you could actually see the data that was in them. With computers, you need to be more savvy.

2. The Varieties of Indexes

At one time, the population of periodical indexes tended to be quite stable. You had your *Reader's Guide to Periodical Literature*, and then a whole host of subject discipline specific indexes:

Art Index   Historical Abstracts
Biography Index   Humanities Index
Biological Abstracts   Philosopher's Index
Social Sciences Index   Psychological Abstracts
Business Periodical Index   Religion Index One
Chemical Abstracts   Sociological Abstracts
Education Index

And so on. The only difference among them, other than subject, was that some offered abstracts (summaries of the articles) as well as citations to articles from various journals while others were only indexes to the citations.

While many of the older indexes live on in computerized form, others have changed their names or combined with related indexes. There are some that are totally new and attempt to address new demands such as actual delivery of articles by e-mail or even full text availability right at the index site. It's now virtually impossible to keep up with the types of indexes available or with their ever-changing interfaces. Staying in touch with research libraries and librarians seems to be the only way to remain up to date. Of course, for many people even the thought of keeping in touch with a librarian is repugnant, despite the fact that we're the nicest people in the world.

Expect change in this area of research, and you won't be disappointed. Despite the fact that it's hard to keep up, the abilities of these newer indexes are amazing and you can benefit greatly from them as long as you keep your wits about you.

3.   Full Text

Ah, the ever hoped-for, ever elusive dream of being able to access the full text of every article you need, right from your computer screen! It could be a reality right now but, alas, reality is never what we hope it will be.

Right now, you can do subject or keyword searches in certain periodical indexes, get a list of articles appropriate to your topic from several journals, click your mouse a few times and have the full text of those articles either printed out or sent to your own e-mail address. The dream has been fulfilled, and you need never stalk through dark aisles of dusty bound journals again. Right?

Well, not exactly. While it is true that some indexes provide a lot of full text, they tend to be rather limited in the number and scope of the journals they cover. Typically, such indexes cover, not just one subject discipline, but all disciplines. For a select number of journals (perhaps 1500-2000) for a select period of time (perhaps the past 5 years), full text is indeed available. But the majority of journals that actually exist are not covered in this way. Once you get into a specialized index like PsychInfo or the ATLA Religion Database, what is available in full text is much more limited.

Why can't every article from every journal in the world be offered in digital form for minimal or no cost? To answer, let me give you a brief lecture in economics. Our world turns on our ability to manufacture things and sell them to other people. If we all worked really hard to produce things and then gave away what we produced, the world would stop spinning on its axis and life as we know it would disappear. Economics makes the world go around. Thus, journal publishers, before they make their material available to vendors of full text indexes, demand to be paid and paid handsomely. Guess who ultimately bears the cost of each fee paid to each journal publisher—the library that subscribes to the index. Thus, *until libraries can find a way to fund massive full text enterprises, only the richest will be able to afford them.*

Even as I write, the company that provides most journals in microform format, is digitizing its holdings. This will provide enormous opportunities for people to obtain full text of articles from thousands of journals. Two questions arise, however: How will this resource be delivered to libraries, and what will it cost?

4.   Internet Indexes

"Why bother with libraries? Everything's on the Internet anyway. Why go to a library to use a periodical index when there are tons of indexes on the Internet?"

Why indeed, except that most of what I just quoted is wrong. There are relatively few periodical indexes available for free on the Internet. In fact, the only really big periodical index available at no charge on the Net is UnCoverWeb at address *http://uncweb.carl.org/*. The reason it exists is to offer you opportunity to buy the articles it cites.

Other than UnCoverWeb, periodical indexes on the Internet are few and limited.

Final Pep Talk

Don't be afraid of periodicals and periodical indexes. They want to be your friends. Within scholarly articles in journals and magazines will provide you with a wealth of current and specific information that you dare not ignore. Just heed the following pieces of advice, and you will survive the periodical maze:

➤Stay calm
➤Stay focused
➤Read the directions
➤Plan your searches well
➤Ask for help when you need it

5

Internet Research

We live in a new era. No longer can we be content to stay in libraries and feast on printed books and periodicals. While these media will not disappear, a lot of research data is now transmitted electronically. The primary vehicle for this transmission is the Internet.

Please supply your own answer to the following question: **The Internet is a world where:**_____

Stumped? Let me supply some possibilities:

The Internet is a world where:

> ➤ you can find information on virtually any topic
> ➤ almost everyone is trying to sell you something
> ➤ you can surf until your eyes fall out
> ➤ anything that's worth anything costs *money* to retrieve (or else you're told that access is "**forbidden!**")
> ➤ you can meet new friends
> ➤ you can't trust anyone or any piece of information
> ➤ you can get your questions answered
> ➤ you can waste a lot of time

Maybe your answer should be "all of the above." The Internet is wonderful and frustrating, helpful and dangerous, beneficial and a waste of time. If keyword searching is the Wild West, the Internet is *Dodge City*. Why bother with it then? Because it is becoming the common denominator of our daily lives. What do I mean? All of us know that most transactions today are becoming digital-we use bank machines, we prefer computer library catalogues, and many of us are shopping from home over the electronic highway. As this phenomenon grows (and it will), the only common medium that can meet its needs is the Internet. It will be the basis, the common denominator, for the things we need to get done.

Thus, love it or hate it, we'd better try to understand it.

> *Disclaimer:* In the pages that follow, several Internet addresses will be given. Addresses change rapidly on the Net, so I make no guarantee that you will find what you're seeking by inputting the addresses given. Sorry , but that's life, raw and nasty, but interesting nevertheless. Check the Internet version of the book (address on reverse of the title page) for updates.

A Brief Introduction to the Net

The Internet has been around for a long time, but most of us didn't know it.

Back in the late 1960's, the US military developed a worldwide computer network in order to remain in communication with everybody involved in the space program and defense research. This network (really a network of networks) eventually came into the hands of non-military people-scientists, computer buffs, and so on. It lacked a common communication language that was easy to use, so only specialists could profit from it. In the 1990's, a common communication language and a common communication protocol were established so that anyone who had access to this network could move around it with ease.

Let's consider some terminology:

Browser-a program that gives you access to the Internet and its searching tools as well as allowing you to manipulate and download data. Two common examples are *Netscape* and *Internet Explorer*. You'll find a browser as a button on your computer screen if you have Internet access. Double click on the button and your browser opens.

Home Page—The first screen you come to when you open your browser. Also the first screen you come to whenever you arrive at a particular address (URL) on the Internet. It is the front door or first room in any Internet site. From there you can click your mouse button on various things to be given further information.

Here's a screen for the browser called Internet Explorer, including a home page. By the time you read this, the interface may have changed, but the basic functions will be the same:

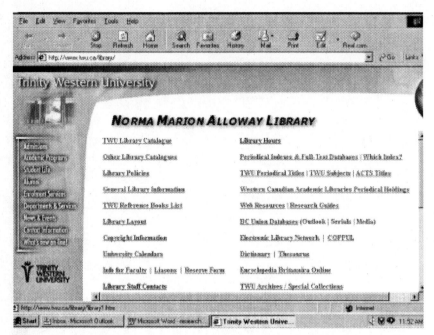

Notice the box in which you can insert an address, the "search" button, where you can find a "search engine," and the "home page" for the library of Trinity Western University.

URL-Uniform Resource Locator. A specific "address" for a database or information site available through the Internet. It's analogous to a telephone number that helps to link your phone with someone else's phone, except that, for an URL, you are linking computers. The typical URL begins with **http://** then has a distinctive alpha-numeric description in which there are no spaces. Thus, you can find the ERIC database if you go to the URL:

http://ericir.sunsite.syr.edu

How do you ask your computer to take you to a specific URL? Easy. There is an address line in your browser. Simply input the new URL you want to go to and click on the appropriate button or press "enter."

Search-Every browser (Internet searching program) has a "search" function. When you click on that function, you will be taken to a "search engine" or perhaps a whole menu of "search engines."

Search Engine-The Internet is a network of thousands and thousands of computers linked, essentially, through telephone lines or other cable systems. Each database held by one of these computers has an "address". But suppose that you don't know any addresses. You just want information on a topic. In that case a "search engine" is what you need. The average search engine asks you to input one or more keywords. When you click on the appropriate button, a search begins through thousands of networked computer databases (actually through the search engine's own indexed snapshot of the Internet, if you want to be technical), looking for the data called for by your keyword(s). You are then presented with a list of relevant database sites, with some summary information for each. You can click on each site in turn, and the information in that site will be brought to you. Thus a search engine is like a servant sent from house to house to ask for something specific that you need.

Here's an example of the best of the search engines: Google. Note the box to enter words, the "Search" button and the "About Google," where you can find searching instructions.

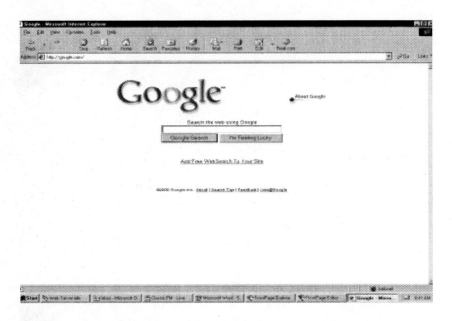

World Wide Web-Also described often as WWW. It is an organization system for sites on Internet, allowing a user with a search engine to
find information from many databases using a common language
(HTML) and a common method of communication (HTTP).

HTML-The common language of the World Wide Web. It stands for
HyperText Markup Language. This is the common language by which
data in the World Wide Web is written.

Document-On the Net, a document is any collection of information
which you locate in your searching (home page plus related pages on
one internet site).

Link-One of the neat features of the World Wide Web is that it allows
you to move from one document to another by way of a *link*. A link in a
document is a word or phrase with colored letters. When you point
your mouse at a link, the mouse arrow becomes a pointing finger. When
you click on the link, you will be taken to another document. Thus you
can move from document to document without typing in a lot of

addresses. This is often called "surfing the net" or "riding the informa-tion highway."

Bookmark-Your browser has a bookmark or "favorites" function that allows you to record the addresses of sites on the Internet that you want to return to. When you want to return, you can click your mouse on that bookmark, and you will be taken to that site without needing to type an address.

How can a person find out more about the Internet?

There are zillions of books in bookstores and libraries on every aspect of the Internet. As well, there are magazines solely devoted to the Net.

Try the following sites on the Internet for some good information on using it for research purposes:

http://www.learnthenet.com/english/index.html

(This one, called *Learn the Net*, is very informative and user friendly. It also has a lot of links to other information about the Net).

http://www.concentric.net/~rkriesel/Search/Strategies.shtml

http://www.concentric.net/~rkriesel/Search/Tools.shtml

Searching the Internet

Searching by Search Engine, Using Keywords

The most common Internet research situation is that you want infor-mation on a topic, but you don't have a specific address. This is where a search engine can help you by taking the keyword(s) you input and searching the Internet for data that is relevant.

There are many older generation search engines still available, such as Excite, InfoSeek, AltaVista, Northern Light, and so on. You can get to them in most cases by typing the name of a search engine, adding .com (with no spaces) into the address box on your browser. A newer generation opened with the introduction of Google in 1999. More on this treasure, available at Google.com, later.

As you will soon discover, each search engine does the job a bit differently and with different results. Some search engines are better for certain searches than for others.

Some search engines *rate* the data they are giving you. That is, they assign probability percentages to tell you how likely it is that the search engine gave you what you asked for. Others do not rate the data.

Some search engines give you *more* than you asked for. For example, they may give you data from synonyms of your keywords. In a situation where you wanted only data that had two specified keywords in it (e.g. automobiles and Europe = an "**and**" search), the search engine may also give you information on "cars and Europe".

Typically, you will get thousands of hits for any keyword search. Thus the search engines that *rate* your data and don't give you more than you asked for are better for most searches, although the synonym function may be helpful at times.

For a solid analysis of several of the more important search engines, see:
How to Search the Web:
http://daphne.palomar.edu/TGSEARCH/

How do you input the keywords?

That depends. Each search engine has its own set of search paradigms. Most search engines have a "**tips**" or "**help**" or "**about**" link you can click on to be guided on the best ways to input keywords for that search engine. Here are some of the common paradigms for older generation search engines:

❖   Use + for "**and**", and-for "**not**". If you do not input + or-, the system sees your search somewhat like an "**or**". Thus:

| +Skinner +behaviorism -Walden | = | (Skinner AND Behaviorism) not Walden |

in a situation where you want information on B.F. Skinner's behaviorism, but not as it relates to his proposed utopian community of Walden II.

If I input

> **Skinner behaviorism**

the search engine might first look for documents with both words in it, but won't hesitate to locate documents with only one of the terms, thus turning it into an **"or"** search.

❖ Some search engines ask you to formulate a full Boolean search, often by typing the linking words in full capitals: **AND, OR, NOT**.

❖ Some search engines allow, as an option, the formulating of a complex search using a grid:

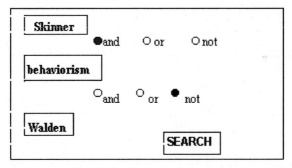

❖ A number of search engines allow you to group words that normally belong together. To do this, use quotation marks:

> **"accountability groups"**

If you don't use the quotation marks, the search engine will also locate any articles that use the two words even though they are not related, as in:

"The president is calling for more *accountability.* This has been rejected by several *groups* of protestors who insist that..."

❖   A few search engines have buttons to aid you in choosing a search. Here's Metacrawler, actually a search engine that calls other search engines into operation, then chooses the best results from each. Notice the button choices under the search box:

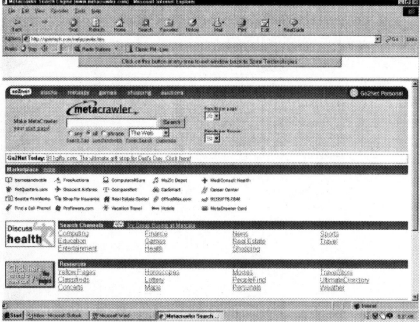

❖   And then there's Google (available at *http://google.com*). At last someone has figured out what *users* want—as few results as possible as close to what I asked for as possible, please. The Google technology, and those engines that will succeed it, search intelligently enough that they do not require the +'s and–'s of the older generation. Just type in the words you want. (Note that Google will laugh at you if you input a +, but it will allow a - if you want to exclude a word).

To quote Google's own press release: "Google has revolutionized searching on the web with its patent-pending PageRank^{TM} technology. PageRank leverages the structural nature of the web, which is defined by the way in which any web page can link to any other web page, instantly, directly, and without an intermediary. In a sense, this link structure automatically democratizes the Internet. It eliminates hierarchy and enables information and ideas to flow unimpeded from site to site."

❖ Always check the search tips for a search engine and make sure you know what you're dealing with. Some of them want you to input names in certain ways. Others want you to use capitals for proper names and titles. Most will allow you to refine your search if you find you're not getting what you want or you have too many hits.

Searching by Subject Tree

All information exists within hierarchies. For example, cell phones are a subclass of telephones which are a subclass of electronic communication devices, of which there are many others:

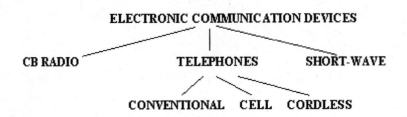

Can you see how such hierarchies can form a tree-like structure? There are certain sites on the Internet where you can search down various hierarchies or subject trees from more general categories to specific ones.

For example, the **Yahoo** search engine, while allowing keyword searches, also lists a set of categories (business, the arts, reference) which you can click on to find more specialized knowledge. One of the most ambitious subject tree projects is the **World Wide Web Virtual Library**. It can be found at:

http://www.vlib.org/

What you will see is a list of categories to search. If you click on one of these broad categories, you will be led to narrower and narrower topics.

Evaluating Information from the Internet

Let's be realistic for a moment (aren't we always?) and ask the question: *Why would people with data put it on the Internet?* The answers are varied:

➢They want to sell you something, and their web page is simply advertising (about 30% of the Net).

➢They have something they want to say, and this a cheap and easy way to do it. Here you can have anything from *"Hi, I'm Tim, and here are some pictures of my car,"* to *"I was abducted by Martians, and I want to warn the world before they destroy us all."*

➤ A government or public agency that would normally not charge for its information wants to make it available. Here you can find everything from the ERIC index to telephone and directory information, census data, and so on.

➤ An educational body that sees providing information as part of their mandate. Here you may get journal articles, electronic editions of out of print books, guides to this and that, occasionally even electronic dictionaries or encyclopedias.

➤ Sincere scholars and other individuals have valuable information and want to make that information freely available for the edification of everyone.

But take careful note of one foundational rule of life: **Few people except the those related to the last reason above provide information for free on the Net unless they can't find anyone to pay for it or they have the financial resources to give it away freely.**

What does that mean for you, the anxious Internet searcher? It means several things:

➤ A lot of what you hoped might be on the Net is not there or you have to pay for it-the full texts of journal articles, the full texts of recent books, a vast array of reference tools, etc. Happily, a recent trend begun by Britannica may provide us with more resources than we previously enjoyed-britannica.com offers its encyclopedia for free and relies on advertising at its site to pay the bills.

➤ Most keyword searches through search engines also bring you a ton of "garbage" that you have to weed through to find a few gems.

➤ It is much harder to evaluate the quality of the material you find on the Net.

Let's consider this latter point a bit more closely. In normal publishing, there are gatekeepers to make sure that material that is inferior doesn't get published (at least we hope there are gatekeepers-sometimes I wonder). On the Internet, anybody who wants to say anything has the chance to say it. Unless it is criminally obscene or racist, no one challenges it. Thus people can tell lies on the Net, and they probably won't suffer any nasty consequences (at least not in this life).

So what happens when you download a document that has no author listed but seems to be reliable information about B.F. Skinner's behaviorism? How do you determine whether it's good or bad information? Here are some clues:

➢ Look for the name of an author and/or organization responsible for the information.
➢ Look for signs of scholarship-good language level, analytical thinking, bibliography and/or footnotes, logical organization.
➢ Look for signs of a **lack** of scholarship-lots of opinion without the support of evidence, indications of paranoia (as in *somebody's out to get us,* or *we're victims of a conspiracy),* poor spelling and grammar, lack of reference to other sources, poor organization. Ask yourself-does this person have a vested interest in promoting a viewpoint or is he/she simply sharing information?'
➢ Ultimately, you may simply have to evaluate the information itself. Does it make sense? Does it ring true? Is there sufficient backing for viewpoints presented? Have you or your professor ever heard of the people involved? Remember that Internet data may lack all the proper signposts of good scholarly work and yet still be valuable. On the other hand, it may have footnotes and a bibliography but be a racist rant. For proper evaluation, the buck stops with you actually reading the material and making sense of it.

Some Internet Addresses Valuable for Research Purposes

In presenting the following addresses, I must warn you again that addresses, like phone numbers, go out of date fairly quickly. On the Net, something you found today might not be there tomorrow. So some of these addresses may not work. If you have a problem, try searching for the title of the source, using a search engine.

❖ **Reference Sources**

The Internet Public Library-Ready Reference:
  http://www.ipl.org/ref/RR/

An index of thousands of books available full text on the Net:
  http://www.ipl.org/reading/books/

The Virtual Reference Desk of Purdue University:
  http://thorplus.lib.purdue.edu/reference/index.html

A biography encyclopedia:
  http://www.biography.com/find/find.html

❖ **Searchable Library Catalogues**

Webcats
  http://www.lights.com/webcats/
(For this one, it's best to click on "geographical index").

Library of Congress searchable catalogue:
  http://lcweb.loc.gov/z3950/gateway.html#lc

❖ **Directories**

American Directory Assistance (addresses & phone numbers-US)
  http://adp.infousa.com/

Canada 411 (Canadian phone numbers & addresses)
  http://canada411.sympatico.ca

❖ **Indexes**

U*ncover* (a general periodical index)
  http://uncweb.carl.org/

ERIC (index to documents related to education and social issues)
  http://ericir.sunsite.syr.edu/

6

Other Resources You May Not Have Considered

Sometimes you get desperate. All the normal research avenues narrow down to footpaths and then disappear entirely. You're running out of time and you have nothing to show for the hours you've spent. Now there's a need for desperate action. This chapter will try to steer you in new and potentially fascinating directions.

Seeing Where You've Been

Before you launch into new sources for research data, it's probably a good idea to rehearse where you've been. Maybe you've missed some important resources. Let's use the following to go back over your research methods to this point and to check possibilities that may have eluded you the first time you went through.

The Strategies We've Covered (Now for the First Time All in One Place):

❖ *Get a working knowledge of your topic* (You went to reference sources (including the Internet) and became familiar with the basics.) Ask yourself:
Did your reference sources suggest other related topics or give a bibliography that you've overlooked?

❖ *Analyze the research topic, narrow it, come up with an analytical research question and suggest a preliminary outline:* Did you set the topic so narrowly that there are insufficient resources? Or did you fail to set it narrowly enough and now you have a fuzzy view of what your topic is? Often a problem with finding relevant sources comes from a problem with being able to focus clearly on what the research project is setting out to do. You need to be able to express your research question or thesis in *one sentence* that deals with *one issue.*

❖ *Do a search in a library catalogue, using controlled vocabularies and keywords as needed.*
Did you find everything that was there? If you began with a keyword search, you need to look closely at the catalogue records you brought up. What controlled vocabulary subject headings were attached to the books you found? (Subject headings are located at the bottom of a catalogue record for a book). If you started with subject headings, did you find all the relevant ones? Looking at the records you've brought up may help you to discover other possible subject headings. Did you consider books that might *contain* information relevant to you? E.g., for a paper on abortion, perhaps some key works in medical ethics might have relevant chapters on abortion.

❖ *Look at bibliographies or notes in the resources you did find. Consider separate subject bibliographies.*

Did you miss anything?

❖ *Do a search of periodical literature.*Did you use the right periodical index for the topic?
Did you investigate the searching requirements for that index?
Did you choose the right keywords or controlled vocabulary
terms?Are you sure you checked your library's periodical
holdings carefully?

(Since every question above seems longer than the one before, I
better quit while I'm ahead!)

Using ERIC

One of the great untapped resources for most researchers is ERIC.
No, this is not a linebacker on a sophomore football team. ERIC stands
for Educational Resources Information Center, a clearinghouse to make
available studies, reports, curriculum helps, etc. that have been produced by educational institutions.

But don't think of it just as an educational database. Educators are
concerned about virtually anything that might be considered a social
science, from the effects of early poverty on adult job performance to
the ramifications of teen suicide. As well, many topics in the humanities
are of interest to educators.

Rather than have schools, colleges and universities put the studies on
the issues affecting their work into filing cabinets, never to be seen
again, the US government arranged to collect them, put them on microfiche, and make them available to libraries. To do this, ERIC needed to
have a two part approach:

1.   The reports themselves. They could be anything from a study
of the effects of TV violence on high schoolers in Salem, Oregon, to
an analysis of dyslexia in relation to reading speed in Podunk
Junction. Normally, such reports would would under 50 pages,

though they sometimes go to 100 pages or more. ERIC documents
(i.e. these gathered reports) are microfiched, and each is assigned a
number for identification purposes. Libraries purchase the ERIC
documents and file them by number.

    2.   A database with which to search the ERIC documents for topics
of interest. Here the government had a stroke of genius—why not put
the database on the Internet so that anyone can search it from anywhere? While would-be readers would still have to go to a library to find
the documents they wanted, identification of these documents would
be relatively easy. Thus ASK ERIC was bornl

    Here's a screen shot of the Internet "AskERIC" site, with the address
(URL) visible (in case your eyes are becoming dim, it is *http://ericir.sun-
site.syr.edu*)

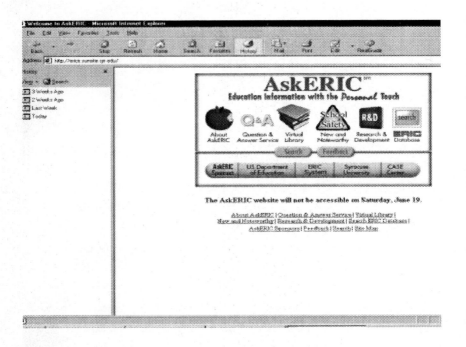

Through AskERIC you can get citations to ERIC documents or educational journals indexed by ERIC, lesson plans, guides, even a question and answer service if you are stumped. Let's consider a typical ERIC search, using the computer screen "search" icon above. When you click on it, you will get an interface that looks like this (although, by the time you read this, it may have a different look entirely, sigh!):

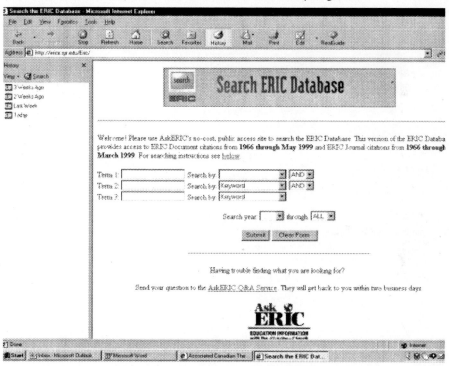

In the screenshot below, you will see the various elements you can choose to search by. Some of them will be relatively useless, but note that you can search by ERIC Descriptor, a system of controlled vocabulary subject headings used especially by ERIC. While the whole "browse" list is not available on the Internet site, ERIC suggests you start with a keyword search, find a few citations and note down the ERIC Descriptors that are used. Then go back and search using those Descriptors.

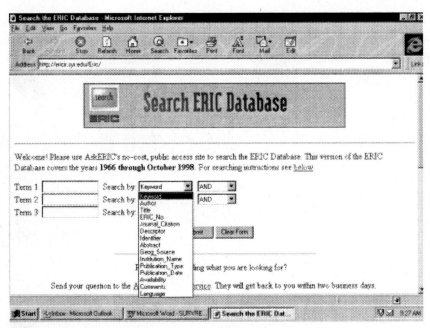

Let's try a sample search.

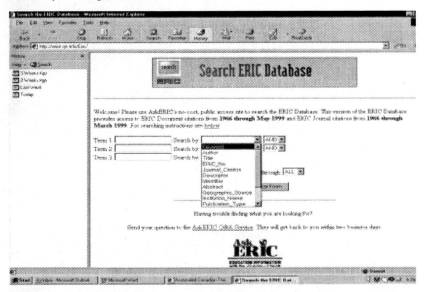

We can assume that teenage depression is a subject of interest to ERIC, since who of us were not depressed at some time during high school, and who of us didn't let our depression affect our schoolwork?

Let's begin with a keyword search, using the terms "teenage" and "Depression." Some obvious problems present themselves right away. The documents themselves may have titles that use other forms like "teen" or "teens" or even "adolescents." "Depression" might come out as "depressed." So at the very least, we need to find out whether or not ERIC allows truncation, and we will need to add an "or" search for the term "adolescent*."

To find out what we can get away with, let's click on the "For searching instructions see **below**." We discover that normal Boolean search terms can be used, but the instructions say nothing about truncation. Oh well, it never hurts to try something. Let's formulate our search this way:

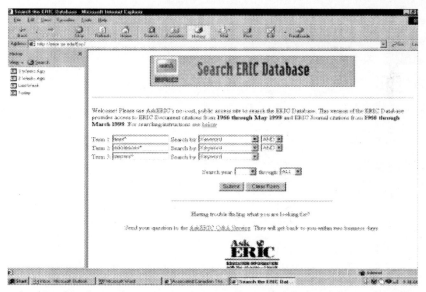

The results show that truncation is allowed. The number of results is certainly workable, not too many and not too few:

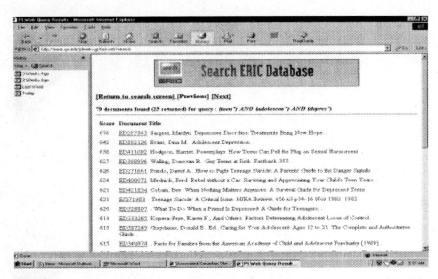

Let's look at one of the documents. A number beginning with ED is an ERIC Document, available on microfiche in a library's ERIC collection. An EJ is an ERIC Journal, which a particular library may or may not have in its holdings. Let's choose the second item on the list above: "Adolescent Depression."

Notice several features of this entry:

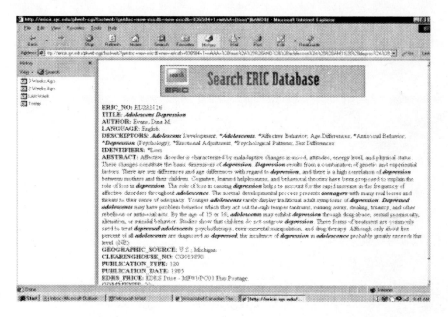

➤ The ERIC Number is first. With it, you can go to an ERIC microfiche collection in a library, look up the number, and find the full report.

➤ Further down, you get a list of descriptors, controlled vocabulary subject headings. In our case, there is no descriptor specifically for "Adolescent Depression." The closest is "Depression (Psychology)." Thus, in this case, the keyword search was more helpful.

➤ You are given an abstract (summary) of the report itself. This is very helpful both to tell you whether or not you actually want to find the report and to give you a working knowledge of it before you read it. NEVER, NEVER submit an abstract as a bibliography item in a research paper. Research demands that you actually read or at least interact with the full report.

Suppose that we decided now to go back to our original search screen with one of the descriptors we found in the above abstract. We could do a straight descriptor search, e.g. "Depression (Psychology)" or link it with keywords:

Here are the results:

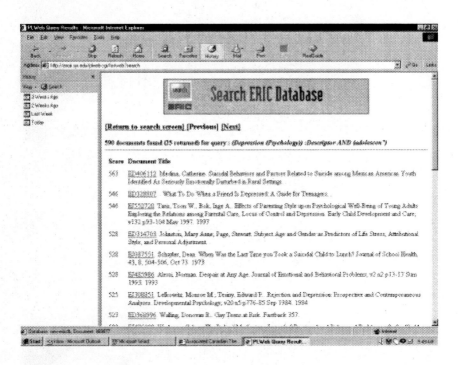

Notice that we got more results this time, probably because the descriptor Depression (Psychology) picked up more articles, even when the keyword wasn't present. In any case, the results look good.

Don't ignore ERIC. It is a very good resource for many kinds of research. The fact that you can access its index on the Internet makes it all the more helpful.

Government Documents

Various governments produce vast hosts of information which is to be found in libraries, can be purchased, or can be found free on the Internet (depending on what the information is). Publications put out by governments cover potentially every area of life. The only problem is that they are *notoriously difficult to find*. If you are in a library that has government documents, rely on your reference librarian to guide you through the maze.

For US government information on the Internet, there is a handy guide at the site: *http://www.access.gpo.gov/su_docs/dpos/ec/tools.html* . This site can help you find materials by agency or by topic. It can even guide you in finding documents in libraries. (In case the address goes out of date, the site name is FDLP Electronic Collection. Alternatively, you can go to the AltaVista search engine and do a natural language search: How Can I Do Research in Government Documents?)

If you are blessed enough to live in Canada, as I do, the Internet site you want is: *http://dsp-psd.pwgsc.gc.ca/dsp-psd/Reference/cgii_index-e.html* . (Trust Canadians to make things complicated—what an address!) The site is entitled "Canadian Government Information on the Internet."

For other governments, try:
http://www.ipl.org/ref/RR/static/gov9000.html

Library Catalogues Other Than Your Own

There are times when you are sure there must be more out there than what you are finding in your local library collection. That's when other libraries can be a big help.

Some libraries are in consortium with others in a local area. They may offer a union catalogue (one search will retrieve all relevant book titles) or they may offer a list of catalogues in the consortium so that you can search each separately. If there is a consortium, that should be your first avenue. Even if you don't have borrowing privileges at the other libraries, it may only require a trip across town to find the books you need and read them on site.

Your library may as well offer inter-library loans at a price or even free. In this case, you can search other catalogues available through the Internet and identify what you want. Two very good sources for lists of library catalogues on the net are:

http://lcweb.loc.gov/z3950/gateway.html#lc on the Library of Congress website, and the even larger site called Webcats: *http://www.lights.com/webcats/* (a hint for this latter one: Search the "Geographical Index.")

Doctoral Dissertations

It sounds so intriguing, so right—if you want the best cutting edge research on a topic, why not locate a few doctoral dissertations? But the realities can be grim.

The searching tool for dissertations is *Dissertation Abstracts International*, a computerized index available in most larger libraries but few small ones. It's fully searchable and you can easily locate citations and summaries of doctoral work on your topic. The problem is that *not many doctoral dissertations are usually available on site, even in larger libraries*. Here are some possibilities if you really want dissertations:

➤ Find out whether or not the dissertation was published as a regular book (some are). Note, however, that the title may have changed, so search by author as well in your local library cata-logue or in one of the WebCats catalogues (see above).

➤ Find out if the titles you want are available by interlibrary loan.

➤ If you are feeling wealthy, many dissertations can be purchased through Bell & Howell: Information and Learning: *http://www.umi.com/hp/Products/Dissertations.html*

If you still can't locate a dissertation, you will probably be out of luck.

Full Text Reference Tools

There is a growing number of reference works that are also available in electronic format or which have an accompanying CD. Each library will have its own collection of such tools. If you are building your own library, you may consider using a CD or even Internet-based subscription version rather than traditional print, as long as you follow this rule: *Electronic sources are best for reference information—short articles, graphs, pictorial data, etc. If your source is simply something you would read anyway from beginning to end, electronic searching of its text may be of little value to you.*

Happy researching with these out-of-the-way tools. They can be a great help.

7

Case Studies in Research

It's all very well to read about the theory of research, but hands-on experience teaches you that we live in a complex world. Methods that may have worked perfectly well in one research project are disastrous in another. Keen minds and brave hearts are needed if we want to succeed in actually carrying out a research project. The moment you've been waiting for all along is here. Let's do some research!

"The Teenage Suicide Crisis"

It is a common fact that the rate of teenage suicides is increasing. For a sociology class, you've been given this topic, and now you're amazed at the possibilities. Should you do:

1. A statistical analysis of the prevalence of the problem
2. A study of why the rate is growing
3. An analysis of the social situations of those who commit suicide
4. A study of suicide prevention methods
5. Any one of a dozen other possibilities?

Before you go too much farther, it's best to get a working knowledge. Let's consider some reference tools, then move on to considering our approach:

❖ **Reference Sources.** After rooting around the reference collection for awhile, I come across the *Gale Encyclopedia of Childhood and Adolescence.* While I thought this was a promising source, it has little on the suicide issue. So I turn to William Damon, ed. *Handbook of Child Psychology.* In volume 3 there is an interesting summary of the work of a researcher named Chandler who shows evidence that suicide can result from teenagers losing "persistent identity over time." He observes that "Even temporarily losing the narrative thread of one's personal persistence…leaves adolescents especially vulnerable to a range of self-destructive impulses against which others remain better insulated." In balance to this view, I seek out a few more reference articles and build my knowledge both of the prevalence and characteristics of the problem.

❖ **Topic Analysis.** Chandler's premise is intriguing. Could it be that teenage suicide is rising in prevalence because people's lives are becoming more disrupted through job displacement, family breakup, youth violence, fears for the future and so on? If so, and if Chandler is right, the relatively fragile self-identities of teenagers may be more under attack. Every disruption results in a disruption of personal identity, leading to self-destructive thinking.

But how do I formulate this into a proper research question? I do it by trying to capture the essence of what I want to find out. How about something like this: *If Chandler is correct about adolescent suicide being linked to loss of persistent identity over time, can the increasingly disruptive nature of modern life be seen as a factor in the growth of suicides among teenagers?*

A preliminary outline might look like this:

Introduction—The problem of a growing rate of teenage suicide

I. Chandler's persistent identity model in relation to other possible models.

II. Disruptive factors which might lead to self-destructive behavior.

III. Analysis of disruption in current adolescence in light of the growing suicide rate.

Conclusion: The value of Chandler's model in explaining the increase in teen suicides.

❖   **Book Search.** Here we have some options:

1.   We could do a controlled vocabulary *Library of Congress Subject Heading* search under the heading: **Teenagers—Suicidal behavior.** That will get us a list of titles like: *Adolescent Suicide, The Cruelest Death,* and *Students at Risk.* When we get down to reading these, we will have to look for references to Chandler's work or to themes similar to those of Chandler.

2.   We could do a controlled vocabulary subject search, using Chandler's name as a *subject heading* to find any books written about him and/or his views.

3.   We could get boldly adventurous and try a Boolean keyword search such as **Chandler AND suicide.** Here, you need to be careful. What kinds of keywords are being searched? Just title words? Titles and authors? All words in a catalogue record? Depending on what keywords are being searched, you will find different resources. I tried this as a title keyword search and found nothing. Using a keyword search which covered the whole catalogue record, I discovered two articles by Michael Chandler directly on the personal continuity issue, in the contents descrptions of two books which were collections of essays: *Disorders and Dysfunctions of the Self,* and *Children, Youth and Suicide.* Without a Boolean keyword search, I probably would have missed these valuable sources.

4.   We could do an author search for books by Michael Chandler. In this case, I could locate only one book, which was not on the topic of

suicide (by the time you read this, he may have written a dozen, so please don't send cards and letters of correction).

❖ **Periodical Index Search.** Here, the first question might be: "What subject discipline are we dealing with?" It could be sociology or psychology or social psychology (life seldom fits neat categories, which is why librarians go bald). Let's suggest two possible indexes: *Humanities and Social Sciences Index* and *PsycINFO*.

I approached the former of these with a keyword search. In this case I tried something relatively fancy: (**adolescen* or teenag***) **and suicide.** The hit rate was 434 articles. So I added one more term to cut the number: **and rate.** This cut the number down to only two articles—rats! Time for a rethink. It is possible also to search by subject heading in this index. I type in the subject heading search **Adolescents** and click on the "browse" key to find a proper subject heading.

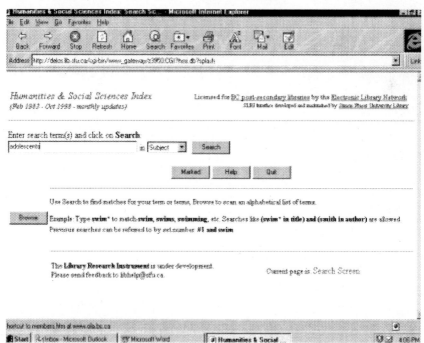

It leads me to two: **Adolescents-Suicide** and **Adolescents-Suicide-Statistics**. The former has 308 articles and the latter has 2.

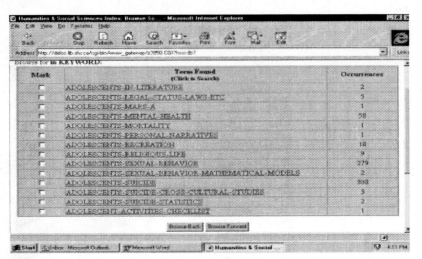

Time for a reality check. While ideally you should be trying to deal with hit rates of no more than 50 citations, sometimes you just find that life doesn't play fair. With 308 citations, you might want to narrow to a recent range of dates. Or you could try adding **and Chandler** to your keyword search (something which gave me no help at all with this particular index).

Or you could move on to PsycINFO. Here, I began with a search of **Chandler and suicide:**

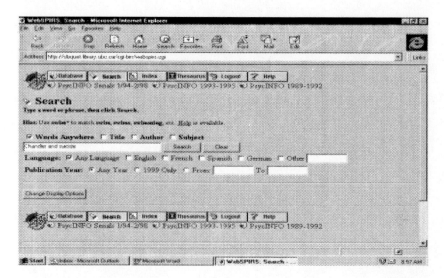

The result was 9 article and book chapter citations, most of them related to Michael Chandler's research. We could go on to do a search on adolescent suicide itself, but the large number of hits would require us to add limiting terms.

ERIC should be the kind of database ideally suited to a topic like this one. Let's go ask ERIC. A search of **Chandler and suicide** finds us only one citation—to an article already identified by PsycINFO. Let's try **adolescen* and suicide and rate**. If that doesn't work, we could search out some ERIC descriptors to see if there is some way to describe adolescent suicide rates better. In fact, a simple keyword search seems to work wonders:

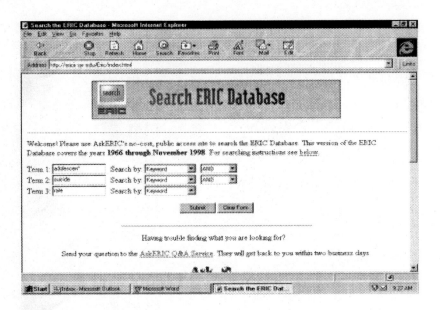

Here's an example of one document citation enlarged for better viewing. While not directly related to Chandler, it shows the research that's being done into the reasons for growth in this problem:

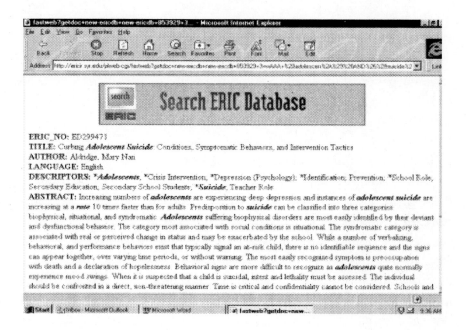

Notice the reference in the abstract to "real or perceived change in status." This sounds a lot like Chandler's continuity approach.

Where are we now? We've identified books and articles related to rates of adolescent suicide and particularly to Michael Chandler's work. Probably the only thing remaining is to dig into the sources we've found to discover who else agrees with Chandler and whether or not there are dissenting opinions. Clearly there is more than enough research out there to provide us with the resources we need. Our goal, remember, is to discover whether or not Chandler's theory is an adequate explanation of the growth in teen suicides.

Let's try one more, this time in the area of history:

"Lucrezia Borgia"

For a course on Renaissance History, you've been asked to write a research paper on a significant figure of the Renaissance period. For some strange reason, you think of the sinister femme fatale of the early 1500's, Lucrezia Borgia.

❖ **Reference Sources.** For a topic like this, any number of reference sources would do, even general encyclopedias like *Americana* or *Britannica*. There are also specific dictionaries and encyclopedias related to the history of Lucrezia's era. The *Britannica* entry provides good background and points out that Lucrezia (1480-1519) had a bad reputation for criminal activity, though it is possible that other family members were the real perpetrators (interesting!). She was a patron of the arts, etc. The *New Catholic Encyclopedia* has a good article on the Borgia **family**, something we will probably also have to study.

❖ **Topical Analysis.** While you could simply write a short biography of Lucrezia Borgia, true research demands more. The controversy over her supposed criminal and treacherous behavior would make a far better project. Why not focus on this research question: *Who was the real Lucrezia Borgia?*
A preliminary outline might look like this:
Introduction (to Lucrezia and her times)
    I. Her reputation for treachery.
    II. Evidence for her innocence.
Conclusion
Note that you will still have to relate Lucrezia's history, but now you are doing it around a definite focus.

❖ **Book search.** Because we are dealing with a person, the task of determining subject headings and keywords is significantly easier than it was with our last case study. Presumably, we can do a Library of Congress Subject Heading search under her name: **Borgia, Lucrezia,** though we may want as well to search for material on her relatives or even on the heading **Borgia Family.** If we find that these materials are limited in number, we might need to find books on Italian Renaissance history, which will contain material on the Borgias.

You can also try a bibliography search. One problem which may arise is that Lucrezia was Italian. Thus, many bibliography sources may be in a language you don't understand.

❖ **Periodical Literature.** Once again, the main problem is choosing the right index to search. This might be *Humanities and Social Sciences Index* or even a more general index like *Uncover* (available free on the Internet). Turning to the former, we can try a search on the subject heading **Borgia, Lucrezia.** Sadly, this pulls up only one entry. A keyword search, just using **Borgia** gives us 12 entries. This provides some interesting results:

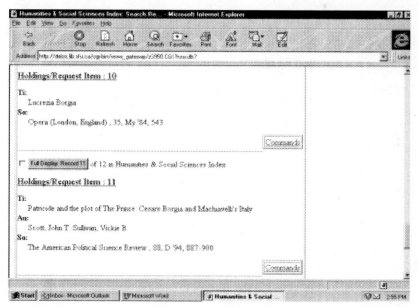

That latter entry looks like it's just what we want in order to study the role of Lucrezia's relatives in criminal activity.

Let's try one other index, this time *Uncover*. The keyword search **lucrezia and borgia** gave only 3 article titles, all related to the opera about her. A search using just **borgia** gave 11 entries, but most were irrelevant.

To this point, our periodical searching on this topic hasn't been very profitable. Let's try one more index: *EBSCO Host*, which also provides a lot of its articles as full text. A little fooling around with this index shows that we are going to have to screen off references to the opera, *Lucrezia Borgia*. How do we do that? Well, if you'll remember your Boolean commands (and who doesn't?), you'll know that a **not** should do the trick:

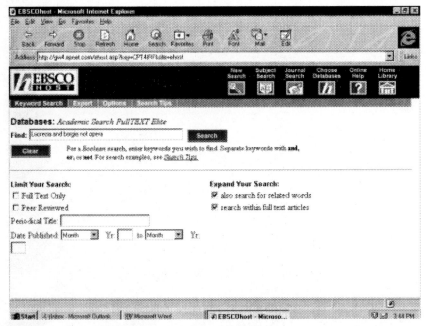

The results of this search are not bad:

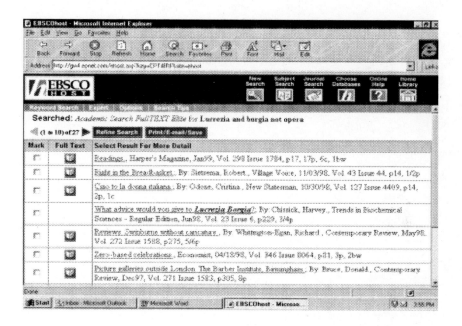

One reference is especially interesting: "What advice would you give to Lucrezia Borgia?" This is a review of a book of case studies in bio-chemical problems. Since Lucrezia was often seen as a poisoner of friends and husbands, maybe this book would give us some interesting data, even if the review is not all that helpful.

Unlike our first topic, Lucrezia Borgia does not lend herself well to an ERIC search, since history is not a social science. Still, there is quite a lot of book material, and we have a few periodical articles that are relevant. This should be sufficient to give us a solid answer to the question: "Who was the real Lucrezia Borgia?"

In the examples above, you probably hoped for easy and tidy results. Research isn't like that. Every project has its hazards and obstacles. There's nothing tidy about gathering information on a narrowed down topic. That's why we've looked at so many strategies. While you won't use them all in every research project, you need to have them in your arsenal just in case your next research adventure turns into a fight for your very life.

Who said libraries are boring?

8

Learning How to Read for Research

It's all very well to amass an enormous bibliography and have all your sources scattered artfully on your desk. But if you're assuming that your essay or research report is now as good as written, you're a couple of sandwiches short of a picnic. Getting the research materials is only half the battle. Now you have to read them. This chapter majors on the tasks of reading and note-taking.

Reading for the Connoisseur and the Glutton

With a tantalizing heading like that, you may want to head for the nearest cafeteria. But read on—food for the mind is better than fries.

Our generation is very big on what is commonly called "escapist fiction." This is the kind of book that makes no claim to be great literature with deep themes but does promise to take you out of yourself and into a far more exciting world.

I, like many librarians, enjoy reading adventure stories, spy novels and such. I've even been known to write and publish such fiction in my spare time. This does get me dubious glances from some people, but I am amazed at how many academics—even theology professors and pastors—read the same stuff.

The advantage of a thriller is that it lets you escape. You can lie back and let it happen without pondering or analyzing too deeply. You just have to let the skilled thriller writer feed you the adventure until you scream for mercy. Escapist fiction is for gluttons.

I do not, however, call a well-crafted mystery novel "escapist" in the same sense. The writer of this kind of work dares you at every point not only to figure out who did it, but why and how whoever did it did it. In other words, such a writer does not want you to swallow the novel whole (as in a thriller) but to read it with discernment, pausing to think over clues with reserve and intelligence. The well-crafted mystery novel is for connoisseurs.

Where is all this leading? Simply to this basic statement: *Research is not for gluttons.*

Consider the problem you face: You have twenty-five scattered sources and seven web-sites waiting to be read. They comprise 3,423 pages in total. At an average rate of one page every two minutes, this will take you 6,846 minutes to read, or, in more familiar terms, 114.1 hours. If you skip classes for two weeks (or take a vacation from your job) and read 8.15 hours per day, you will have it all read. But wait a minute (even though you have none of these to spare)-I haven't allowed you the time you need to take notes on what you're reading. You'd better plan on three weeks.

Before I take you too far into the realm of the ridiculous, I think you can see that there is no way you will be able to read and take notes on 3,423 pages for one research project. The approach that works so well for devouring spy novels—gluttonously reading without thought—is going to sink you when you try to read research materials. There has to be a way to pick and choose the best parts.

Let me show you the connoisseur's approach to reading:

❖ Be Ruthless

You may not like what I have to say now, but I do have to say it. *Any book you read for research purposes must be used and discarded as quickly as possible.* Forget that the author probably worked long into the night to produce the book, leaving a weeping spouse and children waiting outside the study door. Forget that for perhaps years the author was utterly consumed by the burden of this topic until it could be rendered into print.

You need information. The book you are reading has information. The problem is that it has too much information that is not relevant to your research topic. Thus you need to use every skill you have to sift quickly through the material you don't need and find the material you do need.

At this point I must warn you not to show this chapter to anyone with an academic title. Such a person may very well burn this book right in front of you. Professors are purists, and rightly so. They have written one or more theses for which they actually did read all 3,423 pages plus 74,689 more. They got into the hearts and souls of the authors they were reading.

You, on the other hand, are writing a paper that is due, along with two others, in seven days. *Be ruthless*. Read what you need and abandon the rest. It's your only hope.

One big note of caution: I am not urging you to read out of context. You have to read enough of an author's work to have a good idea of his or her main message. It is all very good to be efficient and discerning (the connoisseur) rather than a mindless sponge (the glutton), but be very sure you have grasped not only what the author is saying but why the author is saying it.

❖   **Get to Know the Material Without Reading It All**

No, this is not permission to do skimpy research. This is an attempt to show you how to zero in on what you need without missing anything important.

Here are the steps to take, first for books, then for articles:

Books

First, have a good look at the title page, preface, foreword, and introduction. A book is not just a series of paragraphs. There is usually a motive and a plan, so the preliminary pages can often give you solid clues as to why the book was written and what it intends to do.

Title pages are often ignored because they seem to have so little information on them. But they can be important. Be sure to look at both the title and subtitle, since increasingly titles are there just to look cute, while the real purpose of the book is revealed in the subtitle. Consider these gems:

Lifestyle: Conversations with Members of the Unification Church

Passages: Predictable Crises of Adult Life

Sex in the Snow: Canadian Social Values at the End of the Millennium

The preface, foreword, or introduction will often tell you what the author is attempting to do in the book. There you can look for a theme, as well as for a description of the approach to the subject and of the material to be covered. Reading a good preface can sometimes give you all the clues you need to get into the really important data.

Second, check out the table of contents. This table forms the skeleton upon which the body is hung, the keystone that supports the building, the street signs that give meaning to the metropolis, the—

But why go on? The point is simply that the table of contents provides you with the basic structure of the book in its proper order. Here you find the good, the bad, and the useless. There was a time when tables of contents provided main headings, subdivisions, and even short paragraph summaries of the main arguments. Now chances are that most chapter headings you see will be cute but relatively uninformative. Still, it is worth you while to check out the table of contents. It may help you zero in on the chapter that you really want. And it gives you a sense of the writer's whole development of the topic.

Third, have a look at the index. Indexes can be good, atrocious, or nonexistent. Their real value (when present) lies in their ability to locate specific information when the book itself covers a broader topic. Balancing the indexing against the information in the table of contents can help you greatly by taking you right to the good parts of the book. But beware of two problems:

> ➤ Indexes often list many page numbers after each subject heading, forcing you to do a lot of looking up to find what you want. Comparing chapter headings with page numbers in the index might help you speed up the process by locating the most relevant sections.
> ➤ When you have located a subject through an index, watch out for the natural tendency to take information out of context. Remember that the paragraph you are reading on page 294 was preceded by 293 pages that came before it.

Fourth, be sure to give the book a run-through, even if you are only going to use a part of it. If you fail to do so, you may miss completely the overall intent of the book and thus misunderstand what you are reading in one portion of it. A run-through includes:

> ➤ Reading opening and concluding portions of each chapter to see what the author intended to cover and what he or she concluded.
> ➤ Considering the subheadings in the body of each chapter.
> ➤ Going over any summary or conclusion chapter at the end of the book.

➤ Possibly looking up a book review or two if the book is confusing or potentially controversial.

Fifth, when it comes to reading the appropriate portion(s) of the
book, be a connoisseur of the argumentation, not a glutton who does
not care what he is eating as long as he is eating. Ask yourself:

➤ What is the author saying?
➤ What point of view or background is the author coming from
that might influence what is being said? Thus, what biases do
you discern?
➤ Is the author really dealing with issues or are there some things
missing or minimized in the argument?
➤ How do this author's beliefs compare or contrast with other things
you've been reading? (Here you should be able to group authors by
what they believe so that you can see who supports whom).

And so on. Don't merely absorb (gluttony). Analyze. Get involved.
Ask probing and constant questions of everything you are reading. It
will help your research immeasurably.

Articles

With a periodical article, or an article from a collection in a book, you
lack some of the more familiar signposts—tables of contents, indexes,
sometimes even subheadings in the text. To add to the problem, the
writer may argue a complex point over several pages without stating a
conclusion until the last moment. How do you get a the article's message
in short order and make good use of it?

First, find an abstract if you can locate one quickly. The most generous
periodicals actually provide their own abstracts in the text of their publications. If this is not the case for your article, the article may well be

abstracted in a periodical abstracting tool. With a good abstract, you can discern the author's main points and conclusion.

Second, watch for key propositions. *Key what???* A key proposition, despite its name, is a simple concept. It is *a statement of what the author believes to be true.* Whether or not it is actually true is for you to discern, but it is what the author believes to be true. Most pieces of expository writing have several key propositions dotted throughout with, hopefully, a big key proposition at the end of the article. There are two ways in which an author might present key propositions. Some authors start with a question, then present various lines of evidence, then state a key proposition:

Question ———► Evidence ———► Key Proposition

Others start with a key proposition, then present evidence for it, then re-state the proposition:

Key Proposition ——► Evidence ——► Restated Key Proposition

Your task, should you choose to accept it, is to identify how your author presents key propositions, then *find the propositions.* They form the foundation of the article. Everything else is introduction or evidence. With key propositions identified, you can get to the heart of what the author is trying to say.

[Note: The above procedure also works well with books]

Third, check out the author's ultimate conclusion carefully. What is the author's bottom line? Presumably everything else in the article has some relation to that final statement of belief.

Fourth, if the article you are reading still gives you few clues, read the whole thing. There are times when you just have to muddle through, but it won't hurt as much as you think it will. As you go, try to abstract the article for yourself on paper. It will help your understanding, and if you ever have to refer to it again (in a week, by which time you've forgotten you ever read it), you'll be one step ahead.

A Final Word on Analytical Reading

We have been talking hard realities—too little time and too much to read. Perhaps one day professors or employers will let us work on fewer but larger projects where we have the hours to do the job right. Until that happens, you will need to know how to practice discriminating reading.

Remember that books are sources of data. Develop those skills that will help you extract data with the greatest speed and efficiency. But beware of quoting an author out of context because you did not read enough to get the author's overall message.

Note Taking

We are all aware of those people who never take notes on the data they are discovering in research. Instead, they gather all their books and articles around themselves just before they start writing their first draft, then cite and quote their sources simply by hauling books out of the pile and looking up appropriate passages. Such people, of course, have photographic memories and the organizational skills of Noah loading the ark, or they are really only using one source for most of their data while occasionally referring to others to cover up the narrowness of their approach. Or else (heaven forbid), they're writing their research paper out of their heads and using the occasional book or article citation only as some sort of weak signal to the reader that they did some actual research.

For most of us, it is crucial that we distill out of all we have read the essential things we are going to have to include in our research paper. We don't have the minds or the stamina to retain all we need, unaided by notes, at least not once our research goes beyond four or five sources.

Trying to teach someone how to take notes is almost like trying to teach a baby sparrow to fly. Most of what it takes comes from within you, not from instructions. I can try to help you by flapping my arms and showing you the motions, but you have to develop the will and skill to soar above the clouds.

One of the biggest problems most students face is that they take too many notes that will later go unused. The key to this problem is to formulate and use a research question and preliminary outline as soon as possible in the research process. If you are one of those people who only discerns your outline for the first time as you are proof-reading the final copy of your paper, you have probably wasted a lot of time taking notes that ended up in the round file beside your desk. After all that needless effort, your paper is probably not very good anyway, because its structure was never planned.

Once you have a clear vision of what you want your research materials to tell you in dealing with your question, you next have to decide on a note-taking style.

◆   The Determined Photo-Copier

For some students, note taking is easy. Armed with fourteen dollars in dimes, or a charged up copier debit card, they simply photocopy everything that looks important, take all 140 copies home, and assemble an essay. Would that most of us could afford this method.

A bit of advice here:

➤   If you are using the copier, make sure that you write down the *author, title, place of publication, publisher and date* for every book from which you copy (*author, title, journal name, volume number, date and page numbers* for periodicals). You would be surprised at how many people I find wandering the library, wayward photocopy in hand, looking desperately for whatever source they took it from.

➢ Use a highlight pen on your copies as soon as you have made them, while the information is still fresh in your mind. You want to mark the passages that were of the greatest importance to you so that you will not, sometime later, wonder why you took these copies in the first place.

➢ Remember that your are at a disadvantage if you copy. "Me?" you grin. "I'm the one with fourteen dollars on my copying debit card. I'll have everything done in a tenth of the time it takes these longhand scribblers around here." Yes, but recognize that you have probably interacted with your material at a far more superficial level than have those "longhand scribblers." When you go home tonight and try to wade through all 140 copies, you may find that you have entered a strange and cruel world in which no landmarks make sense to you and the reasons why you made at least half of the copies totally escape you.

◆ **The Note-Book Computer Whiz**

With a notebook computer or a portable scanner, you can input large amounts of material without ever photocopying any of it. Inputting is generally not much of a problem, but retrieval is. I regularly ask students what they do with the material they're entering into their computer. For many, all they do is print it and then make use of the notes in paper form. If this is the case, the computer is little more than a fast electronic pen.

There are some possibilities, however, for making far better use of notes created on your computer. If you can identify key words, you can use a word processor "Find" function to locate those words. You can open several windows of material at the same time and compare them right on screen. You can even buy a specialized student/scholar word processing system like *Nota Bene,* which will allow you advanced file and search functions as well as helping you with the final paper and formatting your bibliography by whatever style manual you are using.

Here is a view of *Nota Bene*'s search function, showing how you can retrieve material by keyword from your notes:

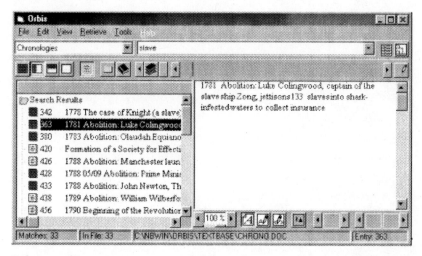

Other such programs are available and may well be worth the investment if you are using your computer extensively in preparing notes.

One word of caution: Because it is often so easy to input notes, you need to be careful that you keep your notes to a minimum. Simply copying everything you've been reading into your computer is probably counterproductive.

◆ Handwritten Notes—The Quoter

Some still prefer a low-tech approach or, lacking a scanner, they are using their own fingers to type material into their computer. At times they will want to get down information that is verbatim—direct quotations. There are some advantages, and (inevitably) some disadvantages.

Advantages

➢ You won't have to go back to the book or article later on if you need a suitable quotation. It will be right in your notes.

➢ A quotation method can give you greater accuracy, since you have the actual words of your sources. This is especially helpful when a topic is new to you. Even when you do not fully understand a writer's argument, you can copy a paragraph that states it. Later, when you are more in tune with the subject, the paragraph may make more sense. If you had tried merely to summarize it before you understood the topic, you may have misinterpreted the argument and carried that misinterpretation into your notes.

➢ The mere act of copying helps you get to know the material more intimately, since copying demands that you read the material more slowly and, in fact, that you read each word several times. In understanding, you will be far ahead of the photocopier when your notes are complete.

Disadvantages

➢ The process can become fairly laborious. It's easier to photocopy.

➢ You must be very careful to quote enough to catch the context. Alternatively, you could summarize the context in your notes, then copy directly the portion that is most important to you.

◆ **Handwritten Notes—The Summarizer**
This person reads a chunk of material, then summarizes it in his or her own words. The point is to condense several pages into a paragraph of notes or a paragraph into a sentence.

Advantages:

➤ This method is quicker than quoting.
➤ The process of summarizing forces you to think about the material and make it your own.

Disadvantages:

➤ The method does not work well if you are dealing with difficult material that is hard to condense.
➤ You will have to go back to your book or periodical if you find later that you need a quotation.
➤ You have to be very careful that you understand the things you are reading. If you misunderstand, you have no way of checking for accuracy later on, other than going back to your source material.

◆ **Handwritten Notes—The Paraphraser**

The difference between summarizing and paraphrasing is that the former condenses material while the latter rewrites each sentence in the reader's own words. With a paraphrase, you can expect that your paragraph of notes will be as long as the book's paragraph, if not longer.

Advantage:

➤ This method can be very helpful if you are working through difficult material. Sometimes just the task of rewriting each sentence in your own words makes the writer's meaning clear.

Disadvantages:

➤ While often recommended by professors, this method leaves you particularly open to a charge of plagiarism (see the end of this chapter), since you are still reproducing the writer's work, thought for thought if not word for word.

➤ The method is laborious. Not only do you have to rephrase each sentence, but your notes will be as long as your original source, maybe longer.

Which Method is Best?
You can use any or all of these methods to advantage. May I suggest that you keep all of them in your toolkit, using each as it is appropriate.

Further Notes on Note-Taking

◆ If you are quoting, use quotation marks in your notes. If the material you are reading turns a page in the middle of your quotation, put a slash mark or some other indicator into your notes to tell you where the page turned in the original. *Always* indicate, at the bottom of the quotation, the page number(s) of the original source you took the quotation from.

◆ If you are summarizing, conscientiously try to work at using your own wording. If you find that your wording is turning out like a clone of the original, then quote directly or photocopy. With summaries, indicate in the margin of the notes the book pages you are summarizing (in case you want to go back to the book later).

◆ If an insight comes to you as you are reading, include it in your notes. Put square brackets around it and end the statement of your insight with a dash and your initials, like this:

[Schwartzburg agrees with Smith on this point. I wonder what Flutnof has to say?—WB]

An "insight" is simply anything that occurs to you as you a reading, as, for example, the discovery that this writer agrees or disagrees with someone else, has omitted something, has made a statement that you would like to challenge, has given you a good idea you want to follow up, and so on.

◆ Make sure you leave nothing out of your notes. Give full information on author, title, place, publisher, date, volume number, page numbers, etc. You don't want to have to relocate a book or article you've already read. Chances are someone else will have it by now and you'll never find out what page that key quotation came from. Other than a cold shower, there's nothing as subduing as having to throw out perfectly good notes because you don't have enough information to use them in your bibliography.

A Gentle Warning About the Horrible Crime of Plagiarism

Just to end the chapter on a cheery note, let me caution you about the academic crime of *plagiarism*. Plagiarism, to put it simply, is passing on someone else's work as your own. The following examples, if they describe your actions, place you very obviously among the guilty. You are plagiarizing if you:

➢ Quote directly from a book or periodical without using quotation marks and a note to indicate that the material is not yours;
➢ Paraphrase an author, sentence by sentence, without acknowledging the author as the source of the material;
➢ Use, without acknowledgment, an idea put forward by an author when you can't find the same idea in two or more independent sources. (The point is that concepts that are unique to an author need to be acknowledged, while more generally used information does not).

Plagiarism is an academic crime because it is the theft of someone else's creativity, because it gives the impression that someone else's words or ideas are your own, and because most astute professors catch offenders quite easily (even those who buy their papers off the Internet), and then feel hurt that they have been lied to. This often results in a zero for the paper and, perhaps, further disciplinary action.

A note on plagiarism for international students—Many international students come from countries where educational institutions encourage copying material from books and articles, then using that material freely in essays without indicating the source. This is seen as honoring the scholars who have written these books and articles. In North America and Europe, however, research essays are supposed to be primarily your own work expressed in your own words. You may refer to or quote other scholars, but you must always add a note indicating the source of your information. Quotations are supposed to be brief and most of your work (90% or more) needs to be *in your own words*. While you may feel that your English language skills are weak, your professor would rather see an essay in poor English that is your own than an essay in good English that just quotes from other sources. In North America, professors value independent thinking more than the honoring of great scholars. Make sure that your essays are your own work.

9

Organizing Your Notes to Write your Paper

"I have seventy-five pages of notes, not counting the photocopy I left on the copier and the two pages which I think fell behind my desk. Now every time I look at these collections of chicken scratch, I want to scream. What a mess! How am I ever going to make an essay out of this chaos? Will there ever be meaning to my life?"

Yes, there will. Take heart. There is a way to organize your disastrous jumble or the chaos of notes in your computer, no matter how incomprehensible it now seems to be.

I hesitate whenever I suggest "my" method for note organization. What if your mind, heaven forbid, does not correspond with mine? What if I am totally out of touch with the logical categories you most enjoy?

Still, someone has to suggest something. Librarians, even though dull, are undoubtedly logical and thus better equipped than, say, Renaissance painters, to suggest methods of organizing information. I am giving you only one method (with some variations) because throwing too many methods at you can be confusing. If you don't like this approach, ask your favorite professor or another librarian to suggest a better one (I dare you).

My system can be called a "register method" of note organization. A "register" is an index list of some sort that enables you to organize data.

Consider an auto parts store. The parts are laid out in bins on row after row of shelves. The fact that the water system thermostats are next to the distributor caps that are next to the spark plugs is not nearly as relevant as the fact that each bin has a number on it.

When I walk in and ask for a thermostat for a 1949 Wuzzly Roadster, the parts person does not immediately proceed to the shelves and start looking. He or she opens a parts book or searches with a computer to find the bin number for that model of thermostat. Then it's an easy task to find the bin with the right number on it and deliver my part to me.

Here's the point of the analogy: The rows of auto parts are your jumbled mess of notes. The bin numbers are codes you insert into these notes, such as page numbers and other symbols. The parts book or computer index represents an indexed outline by which you can retrieve your notes in a coherent way. This is how it works:

Your Notes

Some people write notes on 3 x 5 or 4 x 6 cards. This is, in my humble opinion, a grave error. Even an average-sized periodical article requires two or three cards, written on both sides to summarize its main points. A book could increase the number of cards to twenty or thirty. Not only is that costly, but you know you're going to lose a least a few cards before your research is done.

If God had meant us to write out notes on cards, he would not have allowed us to invent standard notepaper or computer printers that take standard paper sizes. Does not nature itself tell you that eyes, hands and pens were made for writing boldly on decent sized paper instead of scraping one-sixteenth inch high letters on miniscule cards?

Save your note cards for the next part of my system if you are not using a computer, and write your notes the natural way—on lined, punched, normal notepaper. Be sure, however, to follow the right method. As you begin notes on each book or article, be very certain that you include full bibliographical information in the notes (author, title, place, publisher, date, volume number, page numbers).

When you have completed your notes for a particular item (even if those notes are ten pages long), simply leave a few lines blank, then start notes on your next book or article, being sure again to enter full bibliographical information first. (if you are using a computer, see the alternatives below).

One of the important things you need to do is *number the pages of your notes consecutively.* If you have fifty pages of notes on ten pages, then number your note pages from one to fifty (If using a computer and planning to print out your notes, insert page numbers before you print). If you have photocopies, put them in the right places in your notes and number them too. Keep your notes in a binder so pages don't get lost.

Options for Notes Using a Computer

➤ Some people prefer to print their notes onto paper. In this case, the computer is just an input device, and notes are handled as above.

➤ If you are planning to use your notes in their electronic format, you need to determine how you want to set them up. Unless you have a note organization program like *Nota Bene* (see previous chapter), it's probably best to put all your notes into one file so that you can search them with only one search rather than several. The exception would be the situation in which the file gets beyond 40—50 pages. *Make sure you back up your information constantly if it's all in one file. You'd hate to lose the whole thing*

➤ Your word processor's "find" function (often in the "edit" menu) will become your best retrieval tool, though in the organizing process, you may need to input some codes (see below)

Your Bibliography

As you gather sources, you need to keep track of them, including enough bibliographical information so that you won't have to go on a desperate search for a lost date or volume number when you start writing your paper. Here's the minimal information needed:

➤ **Books**—Author, title, city of publication, publisher, date.
➤ **Periodical Articles**—Author and title of article, journal title, volume number, date (e.g. January 1999 or Spring 2000), and page numbers where the article is found.
➤ **Article in a Book**—Author and title of article, title of book, editor of book, city of publication, publisher, date.
➤ **Reference Book Article**—Title of article, author if given (often abbreviation of author name is given at the end of the article), title of reference book, edition of reference book; and (sometimes) city of publication, publisher, date.
➤ **Internet Article**—Author (if given), title, publisher (if given), Internet address (URL), and date you accessed the information.

These days, the most practical way to compile a bibliography is with a computer file. That way, you can put everything in alphabetical order easily, and, if you have enough foresight, you can format your bibliography early on according to the style manual you are expected to use. *ONE TIP*: at the beginning of each entry, indicate where the notes for that entry are—either give a file name (if the notes are in your computer) or page number (if you've got your notes in print form with the pages numbered consecutively).

The alternative is to set up a card file. Each card would have full bibliographical information for only one entry in your bibliography. It should also contain a note on the computer file name or page numbers of notes where notes on that item may be found. Who knows, you may remember that Octavius Flootsnoot said something about the issue you're dealing with. If you've cross-referenced your bibliography file to your notes, you need only look up "Flootsnoot," and your entry will tell you exactly where your notes for Flootsnoot are.

Your Subject Index

Note taking is easy. Retrieval is hard. The biggest problem most students face is that they've taken many pages of notes and photocopies, but now that they want to write the research paper, they can't retrieve the data they need.

Virtually anyone, even a seasoned author, gets writing anxiety—that moment when you are finally staring at a blank page or computer screen (with the cursor blinking in a taunting fashion), and you mind tells you that this paper will never happen. You may have written brilliant papers in the past (or not), but this one simply can't be completed. The fear value is tremendous. Now, imagine that you have the further problem that your notes are a mess, you're not sure you did enough research, and you can't find even the data you remember noting down. Writing anxiety now becomes writing crisis.

The only way to save yourself all this *angst,* is to get organized before you write. Sure, I know you're thinking, "My paper is due in 3 hours. I don't have time to get organized."

My response is that *you don't have time NOT to get organized.*

Let me suggest a method that will break the back of writing anxiety and actually save you time in the long run. Here are the steps:

> ➢ Take a good-sized piece of paper and write your preliminary outline on it, leaving lots of space between each heading or subheading. (You **do** have a preliminary outline, don't you? If not, you've probably already wasted a lot of time researching things

that aren't relevant to your topic, which is why your barely started paper is due in three hours.)

➤ Determine a symbol to represent each heading or subheading. These symbols could be the letters and numbers used in your outline (I., A., 1., a., etc.) or special symbols not normally used in written work: #, $ % + etc.

➤ Read through your notes. Every time you discover data that is relevant to one of your headings in your outline, write the location (page number of notes or file name of computer file) under that heading. In your notes, insert your symbol so that you can find the exact location of the data. For computer files, this is especially important: Later, you can open your "find" function in your word processor, type the symbol (%) in the box, and locate every place in the file where data relevant to that heading is found. Just remember to insert a space before and after the symbol wherever you input it in your notes so that the "find" function can actually find it.

Thus, with this exercise, you cross-reference your notes with your outline. The outline may then look something like this (page numbers referring to printed notes, and notations in capitals referring to computer files):

The Limits of Behaviorism: *Walden Two* in Perspective

I.   *An Introduction to Behaviorism*
4. 17, INTBEH.DOC
II.   *B.F. Skinner's Walden Two*
$ 3, 18, 3, WALDEN.DOC, SKIN.DOC
III.   *Walden Two as a Demonstration of the Limits of Behaviorism*
% 6, 12, 14-17, CRITIQUE.DOC

In the above, note that my symbols are #, $ and %. These symbols will also be inserted in the appropriate places in the printed notes or computer files for easy retrieval of data.

Why go to all this trouble? Simple. It saves time and alleviates writing anxiety. Consider the awful alternative: You begin writing the actual paper and get to heading number one: "An Introduction to Behaviorism." Now you have to read through all forty-seven pages of notes, looking for material on this aspect. Having found your material and written this section of your paper, you come to your second roadblock: The heading "B.F. Skinner's *Walden Two*." Now you have to go through your notes again, for a second desperate search for relevant information. Then comes heading number three, and the whole nasty quest starts all over. In the process, you will have read all your notes three times and recreated your writing anxiety three times.

Thus, setting up a cross-index to your notes before you start writing saves you having to re-read your material every time you start a new section of your paper. Besides, you are left with a warm and comforting sense that you actually know where you are going before you start. When was the last time you had a feeling like that?

Indexing your Notes for Larger Assignments

There may well come a time when you are asked to produce a really large research paper or a thesis or dissertation. Now the process of note organization becomes crucial, because retrieval is much more complicated.

In general, the procedures outlined above work just as well on longer papers as they do on shorter ones. True, your outline itself may be several pages long, and you may have to modify what symbols you use to identify headings, but the same principle still operates—your goal is to cross-reference outline headings to your notes so that as you write the various parts of your paper you can retrieve the research data you need.

A few tips (beyond the obvious that you should always back up your files):

➤ Do your indexing as you are going along in your research rather than waiting to the end and being faced with the task of indexing dozens or even hundreds of pages of notes.

➤ Make especially sure that you are keeping a good running file of your bibliography with full bibliographical information for each item in it. The larger the bibliography, the more the risk of losing things.

➤ If your preliminary outline should change as you are going, don't panic. Go back over what you've already indexed and transfer your old indexing, as best you can, to the new outline. Sometimes this will mean going back over your notes again and re-doing some of the indexing.

10

Tips on Research Writing

Research doesn't mean much if the presentation of your results is flawed. The kiss of death is to have a research paper returned with the comment: "Excellent bibliography, but your argument could have been developed more clearly."

Two problems stand out as the most serious: Getting your outline straight and writing persuasively. Let's deal with each in turn.

The Outline

Outlining is a major problem in any research presentation. If you are attempting (in fear, no doubt) a thesis or dissertation, the problem only compounds itself.

Let's visualize what we're dealing with first, then look at some possible solutions. The reason why the outline is so troublesome is that people receive information in sequence rather than absorbing all of the facts at the same time. Simply because a twenty page paper may take fifteen minutes to read means that some information must be presented before other information is given.

Let's look at it another way. Presenting an argument (that is, the statement of a response to your research question) is like building a house. You have to lay the foundation before you can move to the upper stories. Everything you build rests upon whatever you've already laid down.

Perhaps the best way to learn outlining technique is to look at specific steps and see these illustrated with specific examples.

Step One: The Research Question

As we have seen, the first step toward putting together even a preliminary outline is figuring out what issue you want to deal with. This involves narrowing your topic and stating a *single* research question. For our purposes, let's choose the topic of "Burnout in the Workplace." Our narrower focus will be "preventing burnout," and our research question is, "How can today's office worker resist burnout in the workplace?"

Step Two: Preliminary Outline Headings

Now you need to assess your question to determine what data you are going to need to answer it. For our example, presumably you'll need an introduction to burnout, explaining what it is and raising the issue that there must be means to resist it. You might, as well, assume that resistance will involve recognizing the signs of burnout and taking some counter-measures to overcome those signs or to prevent them happening in the first place. Thus your preliminary outline has three possible headings already: Knowing the signs of approaching burnout, Counter-measures, and An introduction to the problem of burnout.

Step Three: Organizing the Headings

This is usually the hardest part. What you want is a logical order that is helpful to the reader. Above all, you want to avoid the impression that your paper lacks direction or that the directions it is taking are strange and hard to justify. A good outline should not be all that noticeable because your goal is to take the reader from introduction to conclusion as comfortably as possible.

Here are some tips:

➤ Get general and introductory matters out of the way first. Just as you needed a working knowledge of the topic when you started your research, you now need to give your reader a similar working knowledge, including background information and a clear statement of the question you're dealing with. In the case of our burnout example, you would probably have to define burnout, demonstrate what a problem it is, and raise the question of what things can be done to resist burnout in the workplace.

➤ Look for a natural order to your headings, if you can find it. In our burnout example, it seems more natural to discuss first the need to recognize the signs of burnout and *then* to consider possible counter-measures to resist burnout (i.e. knowledge before action seems like a natural order). Here are some other possibilities:

- In a historically-oriented paper (e.g. "The Early Conquests of Alexander the Great"), you might simply want to move the paper along chronologically.
- In an analysis of issues related to a topic, you can follow an ascending or climactic order, looking at smaller factors or arguments first, then moving up to the more crucial factors. Your last section could begin, "The most serious difficulty with…, however, is…" Ascending or climactic order adds power to a paper by leading the reader into increasing tension, much like an action movie builds to a climax. Resist giving away the most exciting parts of your paper early on—if you use up the good stuff early, you'll have little left to keep the reader interested in the rest of what you have to say.

·   If you are comparing or contrasting two or more viewpoints, there are basically two ways to go about it. Now's the time to get your wits about you, so go have some coffee or take a walk, then read on:
    If the two views you are discussing are relatively simple to explain and analyze, try a longitudinal method by which you discuss all aspects of view A and then moved on to discuss all aspects of view B. Suppose, for example, you were dealing with two views on the issue of cloning—**Go Ahead** and **Wait A Minute—What Do You Think You're Doing?**

Your outline might look like this:

I.   Introduction
II.   The Go Ahead Position
        A. All Science is Legitimate.
        B. We Can Trust Scientists Not To Put Us At Risk.
        C. The Benefits Outweigh The Risks.
III. The Wait A Minute Position
        A. Is all Science Legitimate?
        B. Can We Trust Scientists Not To Put Us At Risk?
        C. Do The Benefits Outweigh The Risks?
IV.   Conclusion

You can see that we are presenting one position, then using the other position to deal with the arguments of the dissenting position. Thus the Go Ahead Position will be described as objectively as possible. The analysis will come with The Wait A Minute Position.

But suppose that the arguments are getting complicated, and you're afraid your reader will have forgotten what the first position said about the legitimacy of science before you have time to discuss it in the second position. In a complex situation, you'll need a cross-sectional approach, which deals with both sides of each sub-topic in turn:

I.   Introduction
II. Is All Science Legitimate?
     A. Yes
     B. Maybe not
III. Can We Trust The Scientists?
     A. Yes
     B. Not always
IV. Do the Benefits Outweigh the Risks?
     A. Yes
     B. Maybe not
V.   Conclusion

Now you have the chance to deal with both sides of each issue in turn. By the time you get to your conclusion, your reader should have a cumulative understanding of the issues and of the reasons for your position.

➢   Attempt objectivity at the beginning and do your analysis later. Here I need to get on a soapbox for a few moments:

Why does objectivity come before analysis? Because every view needs to be heard before you criticize it.

Suppose you are doing a paper on the well known (at least to me, since I created him) social scientist Horace Q. Blowhard, who has the audacity to argue that in order to restore public order, the death penalty should be instituted for traffic offenses. Your paper, entitled "Why Don't You Stand In Front of *My* Car, Horace?" intends to rip the man to shreds. But how can you do this most effectively?

If you are still learning the fine points of intellectual maturity, you may want to begin you paper with the words, "Horace Q. Blowhard truly lives up to his name. If there were ever a reason for tar and feathers, Horace (no friend of yours or mine) would be it." From here, your outline would be:

I.   Condemnation of Blowhard
II.   Some of the Most Vile of his Views
III. Concluding condemnation.

But this is utterly the wrong approach. O ye contenders for justice and all it stands for, halt and listen up: *No one deserves to be torched verbally or in print before he or she has been given a fair and objective hearing.* Not even Horace Q. Blowhard.

I know what you're thinking now—When did true objectivity ever exist? All of us are subjective, so why not just state our views without worrying about truth and fairness to other viewpoints? Why try to give anyone an objective hearing? My answer is that, while this is not the time or place to get into the murky depths of postmodernism, all of us know that it's possible to listen to someone else, understand that person and treat that person's views fairly. Sure, our presuppositions will get in the way to some extent, but our goal still needs to be to understand the positions of others as best we can *before* we level either praise or crushing criticism. A good measure of objectivity is still possible for most of us.

Devastating attacks do not come before we have explained the position of our opponents. They come after, when both you and the reader have enough knowledge of the opposing position to determine whether you are launching the right missiles. Anything less than this is poor sportsmanship, bad form, bigotry, whatever you want to call it. Mature writing makes sure every view has been heard fairly before it is analyzed.

Some Tips on Research Writing

This is not a creative writing manual, but there are some things that you can do to give your paper the appearance of mature scholarship. Why do the research if your presentation looks like a dog's breakfast? So read on. There are certain rules of the game that you really need to learn.

❖ **Introduce Your Paper Well**
Introductions serve two purposes:

➤ They give you a chance to provide your reader with a working knowledge of your topic.
➤ They let you state your (*single*) research question. One thing to avoid here–the temptation to multiply your research questions along the lines of:

> "Why, then, did Skinner write *Walden Two?* Did he indeed believe that he could create Utopia with Behavioristic methods? Was he blind to the problems in his approach? Did he later change his mind?"

What you've done is create a shotgun blast heard around the world. You reader has no idea what your real goal is because you have so many of them. The paper itself will be as superficial and as scattered as your introduction.

Keep your introduction lean if not mean. Sometimes a real life illustration is helpful. For example, if you are doing a paper on a historical figure, you might want to begin with an anecdote from that person's life that typifies what you want to say about him/her. Beyond that, stick with the purposes of an introduction—to provide a working knowledge and to state your research question.

❖ **Always Describe Before You Analyze**
You thought I had long since fallen off my soapbox. Don't worry, I won't bring it up again. But do it. Your writing will look more mature.

❖ **Avoid Ridicule**
When you disagree with a certain author or viewpoint, you need to maintain a level of respect and decorum. Your opponent is not a "moron," "idiot," "stupid" or "useless." (Believe it or not, I have seen all of these terms in student papers). This kind of language reminds me of

an elementary schoolyard with two kids arguing about an issue until one of them runs out of ideas and says, "Oh yeah? Well, I think you're stupid." Ridicule is the lowest form of argument. It reveals immaturity and a lack of ability to address the issues in an intelligent manner. Such language only reflects badly on you.

❖ Be Logical

By this, I mean that whenever you are traveling along a certain train of thought, make sure your reader is at least in the caboose behind you. Don't flit around. Don't jump to another track without warning. Always remember that you are writing for someone who doesn't know where you're going. Lead your reader along gently, step by step. Stay on track. For example, when you move on to a new area of discussion, use a transition phrase such as, "Turning to the issue of…"

Having a clear sense of your research question and outline is a great help here. If you have a single focus for your paper, and you understand the steps you need to take from question to solution, it's easier to help your reader along behind you. To make sure you're really on track, ask yourself for each paragraph in your paper:

> ➢ Is this paragraph in the right place in my paper (i.e. does it match the heading it's under)?
> ➢ Does this paragraph contribute to the solution to my research question?

There are times when I come across a research paper with a "bulge" in it. What's a bulge? It's a section of information that has little relationship to the paper topic. How did it get there? The researcher worked for a long time on something that, as it turned out, didn't really relate to the final paper. But no one wants to admit a big waste of time, so the researcher simply plugged the less-than-relevant material into the paper anyway. This turns what might have been a lean and mean research essay into an ugly project with an unsightly bulge in the middle of it. The poor reader is left to figure out what the bulge has to do with anything else.

❖ Be Explicit

I don't know how many students there are out there (good, otherwise intelligent, students) who believe in ESP. They assume that their professors can read their every thought even it is never expressed. Thus we get a gem that looks something like this:

"In looking at the issues of Nicea, we must focus of the Arian Debate. The facts are well known and thus we move to the specific role of the famous Athansius in dealing with…"

What's a Nicea? What's an Arian Debate? Who's Athanasius and, if he's so famous, why have I never heard of him? If you don't explain yourself clearly throughout, your professor or employer has no idea whether you know what you're writing about either.

❖ Aim for Clear Writing Rather than Erudition

The mark of an educated person is not the length of words and sentences used but *the ability to communicate complicated information in plain language.* Be concise. Say what you mean. Avoid like the plague every long word where a shorter word would work as well. Try never to be ambiguous.

❖ Watch Out for Flawed Arguments

These include:

➢ *Misrepresenting authorities.* If you are appealing to someone's work as support for your argument, be very sure that you represent that person accurately. Don't quote out of context, suppress information that would give a more honest picture, or anything similar. This sort of misrepresentation needs to be left to the tabloid newspapers.

➤ *Arguments from origins.* Just because an argument arose from a dubious source does not necessarily make that viewpoint wrong or right. If a nasty government that exploits the poor of its nation comes up with a wonderful invention to help end famine in the world, is the invention of no value simply because the government it came from is exploitive? Of course not. Those who know about such things are going to have to examine this invention and make their own assessment, regardless of its origin.

Similarly, we can't always assess the value of an idea by considering the person who suggested it. While it might seem legitimate to doubt the advice on family unity put forward by someone who has been divorced seven times, you have to look at the person's material itself. The concepts may be sound even though the author does not exemplify them.

➤ *Arguments from Insufficient Evidence.* I am constantly amazed at the way some researchers skip over weighty problems without making their case. They use expressions like, "It is obvious that..." or "Such a view is unacceptable today..." when much more effort is needed to convince the reader that it really is obvious or unacceptable. My reaction when I see statements without sufficient evidence is to assume one of three things: the writer hasn't done enough research to discover that a controversy exists, or the writer has no evidence to offer and is trying to bluff through the problem, or the writer is bigoted enough to believe that his/her mere opinion is all any reader needs in order to be convinced.

How much evidence is sufficient? Enough to be convincing. When you write a research paper or report, you need to imagine a reader who is slightly hostile, who is not prepared to believe you. Then you must present sufficient support for your argument that your hostile reader will at least say, "Well, you make a good case." You don't need absolute proof, just enough evidence to make your view sufficiently viable to be taken seriously. If you don't have enough evidence to do this, then you will have to be a lot more humble about sharing your views. Admit that evidence is scarce and that, therefore, any position you are taking on the matter is tentative.

Sometimes, the evidence is not available at all. If that's the case, admit it. Write something like, "There continues to be much debate over this issue, and no consensus seems possible until more evidence is found." (Do not suicidally write: "I can't understand this issue, so I haven't made up my mind.")

❖ **Know When to Quote and When Not to Quote**
You should quote:

➤ When you want to back up your view with that of a prominent scholar who agrees with you.
➤ When something someone has written is catchy or memorable in its wording. For example, Walt Mueller, *Understanding Today's Youth Culture,* wrote this about how quickly some of today's teenagers resort to violence:

> "Playground and backyard conflicts are being settled in ways that would make Dirty Harry proud." (p. 130)

In one sentence, he evokes the nastiness of violence and makes his point that the violence is often modeled on that of movie heroes (though "Dirty Harry" is somewhat dated). A sharp quote can be gold in your essay.

You should not, however, quote:

➤ When you can say it just as well in your own words.

➤ When the material you want to quote is over 5 or 6 lines long (unless it is absolutely crucial in its original wording and is necessary for the central theme of your paper).
➤ When you already have a quote every page or two in your essay. You don't want to fill your paper with quotations. Your reader primarily wants your wisdom, not that of everyone else.

❖ **Know Some Basic Rules for Quotations**

Make it a habit to present your own material first, then *back it up* with a quotation. Quotations should not normally be used to present new data. Here the issue is one of authority. Every time you present new data with a quote, you are deferring to the authority of your source. That knocks the wind out of your own authority as an author. Let's put it this way: *Who's paper is it?* It's yours. Stand on your own two feet and make your own statements. Quotations are for backup and support. Thus the pattern is something like this: In your own words present some data or a viewpoint, then follow up with something like "As Joseph Schwartz has argued…", then quote from Schwartz in support of your data or viewpoint. Even if you are just presenting the views of someone (e.g. B.F. Skinner), present those views in your own words first, then follow up with a quotation from Skinner that summarizes his position well.

Never, never, never, ever write a paper that strings together long quotations interspersed with only a few lines of commentary by yourself. Such papers are doomed, since your professor knows that her ten-year-old could paste together the same quotations just as well. A research paper is supposed to be predominantly a presentation of material *in your own words*, showing that your can present data and use that data analytically to answer an important question. Use quotations sparingly, merely as support for what you are saying.

If you have a book or article that quotes another source, and you want to use that quotation, the rule is to find the original source that the quotation came from and quote that source directly. The reason for this is that, until you back to the original source, you can't know for sure what the quotation's context was. Only if you can't find the original source should you use the book or article in which you found the quotation. Even then, you need to indicate what you are doing:

3

Raymond Sludge, *The Red Rose,* 47, as quoted in Horace Roebuck, "Roses are Forever," *Flower Journal* 42 (May 2000): 76.

❖   **Know the Uses of Footnotes / Endnotes / Citations**
Their purposes include:

➤   Citing works you have quoted or borrowed ideas from. Most students are aware that direct quotations need to be noted/cited. But you need also to footnote borrowed ideas if they are relatively unique. Here's a (perhaps simplistic but helpful) rule of thumb: If you use an idea that you can only find in one or two of your sources, it's better to cite the source(s). If the material is found in three or more sources and you can't see that these are borrowing their idea from a single source in the past, don't bother with a note/citation.

➤   Stating further bibliography for the reader who may be interested in pursuing the matter. This procedure, which might look a bit tedious, shows the extent of your research and could earn you appreciation from the reader (and a higher grade if the reader is a professor). Even if you are using a short citation format in the body of your paper, you can still add further bibliography as a footnote.

➤   Citing sources that agree with your position. This is especially useful if you know you've gone out on a limb and you suspect your professor is ready to cut it off at the trunk. The support of five other scholars who agree with you may not prove your case, but at least it shows that you are not a flake. Begin this type of footnote/endnote with something like: "So too F.F. Bruce, [etc.]" or "This position is also held by…"

➤ Defending a certain position against possible objections. Here you are not sure someone will object to what you are saying, but you see a potential flaw in the argument. It's better for you to point out the problem yourself and respond to it before your reader can raise it as an issue. A format for this could begin, "It might be objected that…but [then give your response to the possible objection]." This type of note shows your reader that you are not trying to present a whitewash with only your side represented. If, however, you find that the argument you are presenting is important for the whole thrust of your paper, include it in the actual text of your paper. Notes are for additional or less relevant material.

➤ Dealing with a related side issue that might spoil the flow of the essay itself if it were to appear in the text. This use is rare, but you may want to add to the depth of your paper in this way. Be careful, though, that you don't make the multiplying of notes a habit. I recently spoke with a world famous scholar who admitted to me that he has a problem with his use of notes. Only because I'm an overly polite librarian did I refrain from laughing. One of this scholar's most celebrated works was published as two equal length volumes. The first volume was the text of his book and the second was his endnotes. I'd say he has a serious problem (though his notes are often fascinating). Avoid having the same problem yourself.

❖ Watch your Conclusions

A good conclusion briefly summarizes the main focus of your paper and makes your final position clear. Avoid flowery, sentimental, or overly long conclusions. Say what you need to say and end it mercifully. In general, half a page at the end of a fifteen page paper is more than enough.

❖ Give your Final Paper a Professional Look

With today's computers, there's no excuse for a shabby final product. It should have no typographical or spelling errors (use your spell-checker). Find out what style manual your institution is using, and follow it rigorously for title page, outline page, page format, bibliography, etc. With bibliographies, make sure you follow the format rules you've been given. If you haven't been given any, then choose a format and follow it (See **Appendix A** for some examples). Professors tend to assume that a sloppy product is evidence of a sloppy mind.

Research can be exciting, even fun. FUN??? Yes, as long as you see the path of discovery as an adventure. Research can be done well by virtually anyone, no matter what your initial ability may have been.

I trust that I have introduced you to sufficient strategies so that you can develop your skills to do first class work. The next stage is up to you.

About the Author

William Badke is librarian and associate professor Associated Canadian Theological Schools of Trinity Western University, Langley, BC, Canada. He has taught research for more years than he will admit. An online course related to this book is available at:
http:www.acts.twu.ca/lbr/research.htm
You may contact the author at badke@twu.ca

Appendix One

A Tiny Introduction to Three Common Formats for Papers

Over the past few decades there has been considerable debate over the best format for citing references in essays and for the setting up of the essays themselves. The traditional method of footnotes or endnotes with general bibliography at the end of the paper is under serious attack by parenthetical reference systems, which have long reigned in the social sciences. At last report, parenthetical systems are winning the day, even in the humanities.

Two of the three styles below also get rid of separate title pages and all three now use curious names for bibliographies, such as "Works Cited" or "References."

With all this diversity, you really need to discover from your professor or employer which style is demanded by your institution. It might also help to determine how carefully you should follow that form. Some professors (if we dare admit it) are monsters when it comes to form. You forget one period or comma, and the sky has fallen. Others hardly seem to know there is such a thing as a standard style. Being a librarian, however, I'm more on the side of the monsters than the slackers. Style manuals are there for very important reasons:

➢ To make sure you don't forget anything important in citing a reference.

➤ To make sure your reader knows the difference between a title and a name or an article title as opposed to the name of the journal it came from.

➤ To teach you discipline and give you courage to face a harsh and demanding world where no one will appreciate you for anything and every good thing you do will be scorned, ground into the dirt and [but I digress, sorry].

The three standard reference works for the three styles are:

Kate L. Turabian. *A Manual for Writers of Term Papers, Theses and Dissertations,* 6th ed. Chicago: University of Chicago Press, 1996.
Joseph Gibaldi. *MLA Handbook for Writers of Research Papers,* 5th ed. New York: Modern Language Association of America, 1999.
Publication Manual of the American Psychological Association, 4th ed. Washington, DC: American Psychological Association, 1994.

Turabian continues to favor the traditional footnote/endnote system, though she allows for parenthetical approaches. She also favors a separate title page. Both MLA and APA use only parenthetical systems, and reject the use of separate title pages.

The following is a brief presentation of the main features of all three methods. Please be aware, however, that you'll have to look at one of the style manuals above to get enough detail to properly cite a paper. These examples are not infallible. Find out what style you're expected to use, and get the appropriate manual for yourself.

NOTE: In all examples below, instead of *italics,* you could *underline.* Italics and underlining mean the same thing (so don't use both at the same time).

First: Turabian Format_____➤

CHERNOBYL COLLEGE OF ECOLOGICAL CONCERN

ARE PROTESTANTS RESPONSIBLE FOR THE ENVIRONMENTAL CRISIS?

A PAPER SUBMITTED FOR ECOLOGICAL ETHICS 305

BY
WILLIAM BADKE

LANGLEY, BRITISH COLUMBIA
MAY 2000

1

ARE PROTESTANTS RESPONSIBLE FOR THE ENVIRONMENTAL CRISIS?

On March 10, 1967, historian Lynn White Jr. dropped a bomb on the Protestant church. In an article entitled, "The Historical Roots of our Ecologic Crisis." White argued that the Judeo-Christian ethic of dominion over nature was at the heart of western industrialization and has been the predominant motivation behind the West's cruel exploitation of the earth.[1] While White's article has been reprinted extensively,[2] another, even more devastating, essay by Jackson Ice has been largely ignored. Ice[3] listed five causes of the ecological crisis, all of them linked to Christianity and ultimately to Protestantism: Christian monotheism which, in triumphing over paganism, de-divinized Nature; the Christian view of dominion which made Nature into "raw material to be subdued and conquered; an eschatology that anticipates the end of nature, followed by an new heavens and a new earth; the Christian idea of nonprogressive revelation, which works against acceptance of new religious outlooks; and the Protestant ethic, with its scheme of salvation, which sanctioned Capitalism's greed for material gain. Are they right? Do White and Ice

---

1. Lynn White, "The Historical Roots of our Ecologic Crisis," Science 155 (March 10, 1967); 1203-1207; also Lynn White, "The Historical Roots of our Ecological Crisis (March 10, 1967)."Available [Online]:
   http://www.geocities.com/Yosemite/Falls/6185/lynwhite.htm> [1 March 2000].
2. See, for example, Garrett De Bell, ed. The Environmental Handbook (New York: Ballentine Books, 1970), 12-26; Wesley Granberg-Michaelson, Ecology and Life (Waco: Word Books, 1988), 125-137; Francis A. Schaeffer, Pollution and the Death of Man (Wheaton, IL: Tyndale House Publishers, 1970), 97-115.
3. Jackson Lee Ice, "The Ecological Crisis: Radical Monotheism vs. Ethical Pantheism," Religion in Life 44,(1975): 204-207.

2

and the many others who have blamed Protestantism for the world's current environmental nightmare, have a case for arguing that the Christian message is antagonistic to the earth?

In order to evaluate these charges, it is important to begin with the biblical message so that we can determine whether the Christian Scriptures, properly interpreted, do indeed sanction abuse of the earth. Two passages are regularly cited by critics as being at the heart of the problem: Genesis 1:28 and Genesis 9:1-3.

In Genesis 1:28 we see what appears to be a clear

And so on—you didn't expect me to write the paper for you!??

Turn to next page for a partial bibliography in Turabian format.

WORKS CITED

De Bell, Garrett, ed. *The Environmental Handbook*. New York: Ballentine Books, 1970.

Granberg-Michaelson, Wesley. *Ecology and Life*. Waco, TX: Word Books, 1988.

Ice, Jackson Lee. "The Ecological Crisis: Radical Monotheism vs. Ethical Pantheism." *Religion in Life* 44 (1975): 204-207.

Schaeffer, Francis A. *Pollution and the Death of Man.* Wheaton, IL: Tyndale House, 1970.

White, Lynn, "The Historical Roots of our Ecologic Crisis." *Science* 155 (March 10, 1967): 1203-1207.

_____, "The Historical Roots of our Ecological Crisis (10 March 1967)". Available [Online]: *http://www.geocities.com/Yosemite/Falls/6185/lyn-white.htm* > [1 March 2000]

(Of course, the actual bibliography would be larger.)

Note:

Under the Turabian parenthetical system (not recommended but allowed), the format is somewhat like APA (see below).

❖   Instead of a footnote, you use a brief citation, eg (White, 1204).
❖   The bibliography entries are different, e.g.:

Shaeffer, Francis A. 1970. *Pollution and the Death of man*. Wheaton, IL: Tyndale House Publishers.
White, Lynn. 1967. The Historical Roots of our Ecologic Crisis. *Science* 155 (May 10): 1203-1207.

On to the MLA format ——————————➤

{Note lack of title page}

William B. Badke   Badke 1
Professor Flutsnoot
Ethics 563
10 June 2000

ARE PROTESTANTS RESPONSIBLE FOR THE
ENVIRONMENTAL CRISIS?

On March 10, 1967, historian Lynn White Jr. dropped a bomb on the Protestant church. In an article entitled, "The Historical Roots of our Ecologic Crisis." White argued that the Judeo-Christian ethic of dominion over nature was at the heart of western industrialization and has been the predominant motivation behind the West's cruel exploitation of the earth (White 1203-1207; Internet version available).

While White's article has been reprinted extensively (De Bell 12-26; Granberg-Michaelson 125-137; Schaeffer 97-115), another, even more devastating, essay by Jackson Ice has been largely ignored. Ice listed five causes of the ecological crisis, all of them linked to Christianity and ultimately to Protestantism: Christian monotheism which, in triumphing over paganism, de-divinized Nature; the Christian view of dominion which made Nature into "raw material to be subdued and conquered; an eschatology that anticipates the end of nature, followed by an new heavens and a new earth; the Christian idea of nonprogressive revelation, which works against acceptance of new religious outlooks; and the Protestant ethic, with its scheme of salvation, which sanctioned Capitalism's greed for material gain (Ice 204-207).

Are they right? Do White and Ice and the many others who have blamed Protestantism for the world's current environmental nightmare, have a case for arguing that the Christian message is antagonistic to the earth?

Badke 2

In order to evaluate these charges, it is important to begin with the biblical message so that we can determine whether the Christian Scriptures, properly interpreted, do indeed sanction abuse of the earth. Two passages are regularly cited by critics as being at the heart of the problem: Genesis 1:28 and Genesis 9:1-3.

In Genesis 1:28 we see what appears to be a clear

And so on.

Turn to next page for a partial bibliography in MLA format.

WORKS CITED

De Bell, Garrett, ed. *The Environmental Handbook*. New York: Ballentine Books, 1970.

Granberg-Michaelson, Wesley. *Ecology and Life*. Waco, TX: Word Books, 1988.

Ice, Jackson Lee. "The Ecological Crisis: Radical Monotheism vs. Ethical Pantheism." *Religion in Life* 44 (1975): 204-207.

Schaeffer, Francis A. *Pollution and the Death of Man.* Wheaton, IL: Tyndale House, 1970.

White, Lynn, "The Historical Roots of our Ecologic Crisis." Science 155.3 (1967): 1203-1207.

_____, "The Historical Roots of our Ecological Crisis (10 March 1967)." *http://www.geocities.com/Yosemite/Falls/6185/lynwhite.htm* [1 March 2000].

(Of course, the actual bibliography would be larger.)

On to the APA format _____➤

1
Are Protestants

Running head: ARE PROTESTANTS RESPONSIBLE

Are Protestants Responsible for the
Environmental Crisis?

William Badke
Associated Canadian Theological Schools

2
Are Protestants

Abstract

Lynn White Jr. and Jackson Ice, among others, have made serious accusations that Protestants, with their biblical stress on the right of human beings to have dominion over the earth, are primarily responsible for the current environmental crisis. This paper demonstrates that such accusations only have merit if the biblical data is misread. A proper reading of the Protestant Scriptures demonstrates that there is no mandate for humans to abuse the earth, only to care for it properly.

3

Are Protestants

Are Protestants Responsible for the Environmental Crisis?

On March 10, 1967, historian Lynn White Jr. dropped a bomb on the Protestant church. In an article entitled, "The Historical Roots of our Ecologic Crisis." White argued that the Judeo-Christian ethic of dominion over nature was at the heart of western industrialization and has been the predominant motivation behind the West's cruel exploitation of the earth (White, 1203-1207; Internet version available).

While White's article has been reprinted extensively (De Bell, 12-26; Granberg-Michaelson, 125-137; Schaeffer, 97-115), another, even more devastating, essay by Jackson Ice has been largely ignored. Ice listed five causes of the ecological crisis, all of them linked to Christianity and ultimately to Protestantism: Christian monotheism which, in triumphing over paganism, de-divinized Nature; the Christian view of dominion which made Nature into "raw material to be subdued and conquered; an eschatology that anticipates the end of nature, followed by an new heavens and a new earth; the Christian idea of nonprogressive revelation, which works against acceptance of new religious outlooks; and the Protestant ethic, with its scheme of salvation, which sanctioned Capitalism's greed for material gain (Ice, 204-207).

Are they right? Do White and Ice, and the many others who have blamed Protestantism for the world's current environmental nightmare, have a case for arguing that the Christian message is antagonistic to the earth?

4
Are Protestants

In order to evaluate these charges, it is important to begin with the biblical message so that we can determine whether the Christian Scriptures, properly interpreted, do indeed sanction abuse of the earth. Two passages are regularly cited by critics as being at the heart of the problem: Genesis 1:28 and Genesis 9:1-3.

In Genesis 1:28 we see what appears to be a clear

And so on. Turn to the next page for references ⟶

Are Protestants 32
References

De Bell, Garrett (ed.). (1970). *The Environmental Handbook*. New York: Ballentine.

Granberg-Michaelson, Wesley. (1988). *Ecology and Life*. Waco, TX: Word.

Ice, Jackson Lee. (1975). The Ecological Crisis: Radical Monotheism vs. Ethical Pantheism. *Religion in Life 44*, 204-207.

Schaeffer, Francis A. *Pollution and the Death of Man*. (1970). Wheaton, IL: Tyndale House.

White, Lynn, "The Historical Roots of our Ecologic Crisis. (1967)." *Science 155* (3767): 1203-1207.

_____. (1967, 10 March) The Historical Roots of our Ecological Crisis. http://www.geocities.com/Yosemite/Falls/6185/lynwhite.htm [1 March 2000].

(Of course, the actual bibliography would be larger.)

Appendix Two

The International Student's Guide to North American Academic Libraries

An academic library is a useful source of information for students who are doing assigned readings and research essays. Yet the library is also a place of worry, even of fear, for many students. This manual will explain the basic features of North American academic libraries in order to reduce that worry and help you to use a library more effectively.

The Purpose of an Academic Library

Many students think of a library as a collection of books and journals. If you are an international student, you may never have seen so many books and journals in one place before. Your first questions may be: "Where do I begin? How can I possibly find what I need?"

Rather than thinking of the library as a *collection* of printed materials, it is better to think of the library as a source of *information*. That information may be found in books or journals or audio cassettes or videos. The important thing to remember is that you are looking for *information*.

In the library, there are ways to locate that information more easily. If you understand these ways, using a library will not be as difficult as you thought it would be.

The Parts of an Academic Library

Before we look at methods to find the information you need, it is important to understand where you are going. Let us take a tour of an average academic library:

❖   **Circulation Counter**

As you enter a library, you will probably see a counter with people behind it. This is the place where you will sign out the books you want to take with you. More about this counter and how to sign out books will be found below.

❖   **The Catalogue**

The catalogue is usually near the entrance of the library as well. What is a catalogue? It is an index of names, titles and subjects related to the book collection in the library you are using. Think of it as a guide to help you locate books that you need.

These days, almost all catalogues are in computer format, though you may experience a library that still has a card catalogue. Further below, you will receive instruction on how to use a library catalogue.

❖   **The Reference Collection**

As you move further into the library, you will find an area labelled "Reference Books" or "Reference Collection." These are books that are to be consulted within the library only. In most cases you cannot sign them out and take them home.

What are reference books? They are dictionaries, encyclopaedias, handbooks, manuals, atlases, and so on. Each has been produced to allow the user to look up brief information.

You are probably familiar with word dictionaries that allow you to look up definitions or translate from one language to another. But there are also dictionaries and encyclopaedias on almost any subject you could imagine—religion, psychology, sociology, history, and many others. These reference books are concerned with more than just the meanings of words. They explain the major concepts and people involved with particular subjects.

For example, in a dictionary or encyclopaedia of psychology, you might look up "behaviorism" or "personality theories" or "Freud, Sigmund," and find a paragraph or even several pages that explain each subject. In a dictionary of theology, you might find "atonement" or "Calvinism" or "Thomas Aquinas," and some brief information that explains each of these.

The advantage of reference books is that they give you enough basic information about a topic to help you search intelligently for more information. As well, an article in a reference book will often explain the important controversies and questions involved in that topic.

❖   The Circulating Collection

This is usually the largest part of the library collection. It consists of books that can be signed out and taken home.

If you are used to a small library, you probably found books by walking through the library and looking at the shelves until you saw what you wanted. *This is not a useful method in a larger academic library. There are too many books, and you will only waste your time.*

If you want to find the books you need easily, you will have to use the catalogue. More information on use of the catalogue will be provided below.

❖   The Periodical Collection

Periodicals are magazines and journals that are delivered to the library at regular intervals—daily, weekly, monthly, quarterly or annually. You've already experienced periodicals, even if you've only read a newspaper or *Time Magazine.*

Most libraries collect and bind their periodicals by title, so that they may have many years of a magazine or journal bound in several volumes. Many libraries have older years of journals only in microfiche or microfilm forms. You will need to use a microfiche or microfilm reader to read them. Most libraries also have reader-printers to copy microfiche or microfilm onto printers. A microfiche looks like a photographic negative except that it is on a sheet that is about 4" X 6" in size. If you hold a microfiche up to the light, you will see that it is information printed in very small letters, too small to read unless you use a microfiche reader, which is a machine that projects the microfiche image in magnified form on a screen. Microfilm is in a roll rather than a flat sheet, and needs its own special machine in order for you to read it. *If you have difficulty using microfiche or microfilm, ask a librarian for assistance.*

Many libraries now have the full text of some periodicals in computerised form, often as part of a periodical index. We will be looking at periodical indexes soon (see below)

An academic library will usually have a catalogue to the periodicals that it collects, listing which periodicals the library has and what years and volumes are available. The catalogue will tell you if the periodical comes in normal paper form or is in microfiche or microfilm. Where will you find such a catalogue? Some libraries have it in computerised form. Others use a booklet or a card file to indicate which periodicals it has. *If you cannot locate the periodical catalogue, ask a reference librarian.*

Here are some things you should know about periodicals:

➤ Most periodical publishers assign a volume number to their periodical for each year it is published. Thus the first year of a periodical will be volume 1, the second year volume 2, and so on.

➤ Each issue of a periodical is also numbered. Thus you will have volume 1, issue 1; volume 1, issue 2; volume 1, issue 3; and so on.

➤ Some periodicals begin each new issue with page 1. Others continue the numbering right through all the issues of the year. Thus issue 1 might end on page 117. Issue 2 will begin on page 118. If it ends on page 236, issue 3 will begin on page 237. The reason some periodicals do this is that they expect the library to bind the whole year's issues at the end of the year. When it is bound, the volume will be numbered in order, from page 1 to page 436.

➤ There is no library that has all the periodical titles that are published. In every library, you will find only *some* of all the periodicals available in the world.

❖ **Periodical Indexes**

How does a person find periodical articles on a particular topic? One method might be to look at many periodical issues, hoping that one of them will have an article that is suitable for the topic. But that method could take a very long time.

The other way is to consult a periodical index. Periodical indexes do for periodical articles what the book catalogue does for the library— they provide an index so that you can search for articles by subject no matter what journal or magazine contains these articles.

There are general periodical indexes which deal with many topics, and also indexes which are specially designed for various subject disciplines: Psychology, Sociology, Literature, History, Religion, and so on.

Most indexes, these days, are in computerised form. You can enter subject words or key words, and you will be provided with a list of articles from many journals. NOTE: *It is very important to take note at least of the title of the Journal (e.g.* Journal of the American Scientific Affiliation), *the journal volume, and the page numbers where the article is to be found.*

A number of periodical indexes today offer you the full text of the articles you locate, in computerised form. You can print the articles or send them to your e-mail address.

❖   **Other Materials**
Your library will probably have audio cassettes and videos available, as well as government documents and various special collections. Ask the reference librarian to tell you what materials of these types are available. There are specialised indexes available for some of these materials, and instruction from a librarian is necessary.

Using the Library Catalogue

Most library catalogues are now in computer format. Here are some of the basic facts that you need to know:

❖   **The Catalogue Record**
Here is a sample catalogue record such as you might find in a computerised library catalogue:

Call Number	Z710 .B23 1990
Title	The survivor's guide to library research /
Author	Badke, William B., 1949-
Publisher	Grand Rapids, Mich. : Zondervan Pub. House : Academic and Professional Books, c1990.
Description	125 p.: ill. ; 24 cm.
ISBN	031053111X
Subject(s)	Libraries and readers—Handbooks, manuals, etc.
	Libraries and students—Handbooks, manuals, etc.
	Bibliography—Methodology—Handbooks, manuals, etc.
	Research—Methodology—Handbooks, manuals, etc.
	Report writing—Handbooks, manuals, etc.

What you have in a catalogue record is all the information you need to locate the book. The *call number* is especially important. This will be the number on the spine of the book when you find it on the shelf. (More information on call numbers is provided below.)

❖   **Searching for Books in a Library Catalogue**
See Chapter 2: "Databases" for information about controlled vocabularies, keywords and Boolean searching. The important thing to remember is that with a computer catalogue, you can usually search for anything that is in a catalogue record. Thus, if you want to find a book by someone named "Badke," you can type in his name as an "author" search. If you know the book you are looking for is *The Survivor's Guide to Library Research,* you can type that title as a title search. If you are looking for books on library research, you could type "library research" as a keyword search. In each case, the catalogue would give you the catalogue record above.

There are many different kinds of computer catalogues. Each of them will look different on the computer screen, but each of them does the same thing—provide you with an index so that you can search for the book you want and get a call number from the catalogue record so that you can find the book on the library shelf. When you come to a type of catalogue which you haven't seen before, *it is very important to read the instructions on the screen or to find a nearby instruction manual or to ask a reference librarian for help.* Don't spend hours becoming worried because you can't understand how to use the computer. Look for written guideliness or for a reference librarian to help you.

❖   **Classification Systems**
There are two classification systems most commonly in use in North America—*Dewey Decimal Classification* and *The Library of Congress Classification System.* Before we look at each, let us see what a classification system does.

We saw that the catalogue can tell you if a book by a certain author or having a certain title is in the library. You can also search for subject headings or keywords to get a list of the library's books on a certain topic. But how do we actually locate those books in the library? If a library has only 200 volumes, this is not too much of a problem. You simply look through the 200 books until you find the ones you want. To help you, the library could arrange all its books on the shelves alphabetically by author. Or it could assign a number to each book as it came into the collection. Then if you wanted *Survivor's Guide to Library Research*, you could note from the catalogue record that it is book number 186, and you could just go along the shelves until you got to the 186th book. It would have a 186 on its spine.

But there is a reason why libraries are not organised by the author's name or by book numbers—Students like to see books on the same topic *grouped together*. For example, all the books about Sigmund Freud should be on the same shelf.

Small libraries could arrange their books by broad subjects—the sociology books here and the psychology books over there. But as libraries grow bigger, it becomes more difficult to find what you want. Classification systems have been developed *to help a library to group similar books together* so that students can see several books on their topic all in the same place.

Both of the classification systems we will be discussing below began in the same way: They divided up all of knowledge into a number of headings and assigned letters and/or numbers to each heading. Let's look at each one:

➤The Library of Congress Classification System

This system begins with one or two letters of the alphabet, followed by numbers. An example would be BL625.

The alphabet letter(s) tell you what the broad subject is, as follows:

A   General Works

B-BJ Philosophy, Psychology

BL-BX Religion

C   Auxiliary Sciences of History

D   History: General and Old World (Eastern Hemisphere)

E-F   History: America (Western Hemisphere)

G   Geography, Anthropology, Recreation

H   Social Sciences

J   Political Science

KD   Law of the United Kingdom and Ireland

KF   Law of the United States

L   Education

M   Music

N   Fine arts

P-PA General philology and linguistics

       Classical languages and literature

PB-PH Modern European languages

PJ-PM Languages and literatures of Asia, Africa, Oceania, American

       Indian languages, artificial languages

(There are further language subdivisions for **PN-PT**, which are not listed here)

Q   Science

R   Medicine

S   Agriculture

T   Technology

U   Military Science

V   Naval Science

Z   Bibliography, Library science

To find a book with the classification number BL625, you must go to the part of the library where the B's begin, then move along the shelves until you reach the BL's (the signs at the end of each row should help you to find the area you want). Then move along the BL's until you find BL625.

You will notice on the catalogue record that you do not just have a classification number to look up (such as BL625), but other things as well, for example BL625 .W42 1998. If you were to see that whole number on the spine of a book, it might be printed as:

```
BL
625
.W42
1999
```

While BL625 was a classification number, BL625 .W42 1998 is referred to as a *call number*. In a larger library, the call number gives additional information so that you can locate the right book. If you go to the section of the library that has books with BL625 on their spines, you will find that there are several such books. The library needs to arrange these in some kind of order. What most libraries have chosen is a *cutter* system, a letter and number system that is alphabetical and is usually based on the author's last name. Thus, when you get to the BL625's, you need to look at the next line, lower on the spine. By reading the letters in alphabetical order, you can locate .W42.

Here is how it works. Imagine that you have come to the BL625 section of the library, and there are several books with the same BL625. They will be arranged in alphabetical order as follows—notice how the *cutter* tells you the order, first by the letter used, and then by the number:

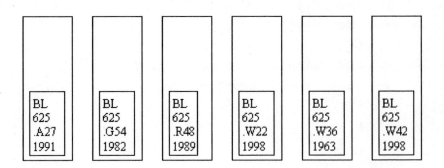

The date is generally not very important, except when you have two editions of the same book.

➤Dewey Decimal Classification

Dewey Decimal Classification uses only numbers for its classification plan. It divides all knowledge like this:

000   Generalities
100   Philosophy and related disciplines
200   Religion
300   Social sciences
400   Language
500   Pure sciences
600   Technology (Applied sciences)
700   The arts   Fine and decorative arts
800   Literature
900   General geography and history and their auxiliaries

Within each of the 100 numbers, the Dewey system subdivides knowledge in that discipline even further. For example, part of the 900 (geography and history) section includes these numbers:

900 General geography and history
910 General geography   Travel
913 Geography of the ancient world
930 General history of the ancient world
940 General history of Europe
950 General history of Asia
951 China & adjacent areas
952 Japan & adjacent islands
954 South Asia   India
and so on.

Because there is so much knowledge in the world, further sub-divisions were needed. Thus, Dewey added decimal points and then more numbers, sometimes a lot of them. The culture of ancient Egypt, for example, is 913.32, and the Habsburg rulers of Austria are 943.604.

It is easy to find most books with Dewey Decimal numbers, as long as you remember the following:

1.   You must begin with the first three numbers of the classification number and locate that place on the shelves. If there is a decimal point and more numbers, then move along the shelves to your *right* until you find the right classification.

2.   A classification number in Dewey may be so long that it continues on the next line. Thus 227.1077 may look like this on the spine of the book:

227.1

077

3.   Dewey Decimal Classification uses the same *cutter* method that Library of Congress uses (see section A. above). Thus you will find that the catalogue will show a number like this: 226.067 .H272 1997, which on the spine of the book will look like this:

```
226.067
.H272
1997
```

Dewey Decimal numbers are *decimal*. Thus they run in this order:
306.7
306.72
306.724
306.8
306.85
306.9

Signing Out Books

When you want to borrow books to take with you, you need to know the rules for taking out books. Each library has its own set of rules, and so you must obtain and read the regulations provided by that library.
Here are some procedures and suggestions:

➤ In most libraries, certain books can be signed out (borrowed) and certain books cannot. Usually reference books cannot be signed out. In many libraries, periodicals cannot be signed out. If you are in doubt, read the library regulations or ask someone at the circulation desk.

➤ If you want to borrow books, you will need to find them yourself and bring them to the circulation desk. Normally, you will have to show a borrower's card *for that library* in order to borrow books. If you are using a library for which you do not have a card, you may need to pay money to obtain one.

> ➤ When you sign out a book, you may have to sign your name on a card, or your name may be entered automatically into a computer. If you do not know how to sign out a book, just tell the staff member that you have not signed out books there before. The staff member will tell you what to do.
> ➤ Many colleges and universities also have a selection of *reserve* materials which are normally held at the circulation desk. These are materials that a professor wants all of his or her students to use. These books or articles have a short borrowing period, which may be as long as three days or as short as two hours. Usually the professor will tell the student which books have been placed on reserve. You may then ask at the circulation desk for the books you need, and borrow them for the length of time indicated.
> ➤ Be sure to notice when your books are to be returned. Record that date on your calendar so that you will remember when to return your books. If you are done with your books earlier than this date, you should return them early so that others may use them. Often you can renew your books (sign them out again) one or two times. If you return your books late, however, you will have to pay a fine. Returning books late is unkind to other students who may have been waiting to use those books.

Some Words about Plagiarism

In many countries, teachers and professors encourage their students to copy information from books and present that information in an essay without writing down where that information came from. Often this means that an essay is a collection of quotations from various books, with little or no information in the essay actually created by the student.

In North America, that kind of essay is *not acceptable*. Professors want to see your own thoughts and words. While you may quote from books and periodicals, you must always indicate in a footnote or end-note where the quotation came from. If you do not, you are committing *plagiarism*.

What is *plagiarism?*—*Plagiarism is writing down someone else's words or ideas as if they were your own.* If you take a quotation from a book and write it in your essay, you must put quotation marks around it and use a note to indicate where you got that quotation. Even if you take sentences from a book and rewrite them in your own words, this is plagiarism. One further example of plagiarism is having someone else write your essay for you.

In North America, plagiarism is seen as stealing someone else's words or ideas and presenting them as your own. It is considered *very* serious and will usually result in a zero for your essay as well as further disciplinary action.

Some Final Advice

❖ If you are not familiar with the library you are using, take this manual with you and *explore* the library. Locate all the parts of it—circulation desk, catalogue, reference collection, and so on. Spend an hour getting to know the library as well as you can.

❖ Never be afraid to ask library staff for help. Part of their job is to help students, and they are very good at answering questions.

❖ Do not let a fear of libraries stop you from enjoying them. Most students feel nervous in a library at first. The more time you spend in the library, the easier it will be to use.